TRUE CRIME STORIES

3 True Crime Books Collection

By
Jack Rosewood

Copyright © 2016 by LAK Publishing

ALL RIGHTS RESERVED

No part of this book may be reproduced, stored in a retrieval system, or transmitted in any form or by any means, electronic, mechanical, photocopying, recording, scanning, or otherwise, without the prior written permission of the publisher.

DISCLAIMER:

This crime anthology biography includes quotes from those closely involved in the twelve cases examined, and it is not the author's intention to defame or intentionally hurt anyone involved. The interpretation of the events leading up to these crimes are the author's as a result of researching the true crime murders. Any comments made about the psychopathic or sociopathic behavior of criminals involved in any of these cases are the sole opinion and responsibility of the person quoted.

FREE BONUS!

Get two free books when you sign up to my VIP newsletter at www.jackrosewood.com/free 150 interesting trivia about serial killers and the story of serial killer Herbert Mullin.

CONTENTS

TRUE CRIME STORIES VOLUME 1 1

Introduction 3

CHAPTER 1: A Killer Coincidence? The Mary Morris Murders .. 5

    Mary Henderson Morris 6

    Mary McGinnis Morris 8

    Suspects and Theories 8

    A Hit Gone Wrong? 13

CHAPTER 2: The Disappearances of the Palmer Brothers 15

    A Family of Men 16

    The Disappearance of Michael 17

    The Disappearance of Chucky Palmer 19

CHAPTER 3: The Liquid Matthew Case 22

    A Body and Cryptic Clues 23

    The Explanation 25

CHAPTER 4: The Brighton Trunk Murders 26

    The "Queen of Watering Places" 26

    The 1831 Murder 27

    Minnie Bonati 28

    The "Girl with the Pretty Feet" 30

    The Murder of Violette Kay/Saunders 32

CHAPTER 5: The Abduction and Murder of Annie Le 36

    A Woman with a Promising Future 37

    The Crime 38

    The Killer 40

    Unanswered Questions 42

    An Eerie Footnote 44

CHAPTER 6: The Disappearance of the McStay Family 45

    The Disappearance 46

    Media Attention and Investigation 49

    A Suspect Emerges 51

    The Discovery 53

CHAPTER 7: The Rayna Rison Murder 56

    A Promising Future 57

    The Search for Rayna 58

    The Case Goes Cold 59

    Old Loyalties are Shattered 62

CHAPTER 8: The Murder of Sara Lynn Wineski 68

    Sara Lynn Wineski 69

    A DNA Match 70

CHAPTER 9: The Murder of Little Anna Palmer 74

    The Crime 75

    The Investigation 76

    Matt Breck... 78

CHAPTER 10: The Strange Murder of Roy McCaleb 81

    A Carjacking and a Murder 81

    The Years Pass By... 84

CHAPTER 11: Robert Zarinsky – A Serial Killer Nabbed by DNA 87

    A Predator from the Beginning 88

    A Life of Murder and a Life in Prison.................................... 89

    Science Identifies a Serial Killer 91

CHAPTER 12: The Murder of Patricia Beard............................ 96

    The Denver Cold Case Unit... 98

Conclusion 101

TRUE CRIME STORIES VOLUME 2 103

Introduction... 105

CHAPTER 1: Murder in the French Alps – Iqbal Al-Hilli and her Family 107

    From Scenic Views to Crime Scene 107

    A Puzzle with Too Many Angles 108

    Saad Al-Hilli 108

    Sylvain Mollier... 109

    The Work of a Serial Killer? 110

    Mystery Motorcyclist.. 110

    The Legionnaire 110

    Iqbal Al-Hilli 110

    A Secret Husband? 111

    Death by Coincidence 112

    Murder Unsolved 113

CHAPTER 2: The Villisca Axe Murders 115

    The Moore's 115

    A Gruesome Scene 116

    Who Were the Suspects? 118

    Fourteen Witnesses Called to Coroner's Inquest 123

    Deathbed and Jailhouse Confessions 125

CHAPTER 3: The Disappearance of Stacy Peterson and
Christie Marie Cales 128

    The Troubled Life of Stacy 128

    Gone Without a Trace 130

    Morphey's Story 131

    Kathleen Savio 133

    Another Wife Murdered? The Trial of Drew Peterson 134

    Disappearance of Her Mother—Christie Marie Cales 135

CHAPTER 4: Lucia de Berk – Angel of Death? 138

    Accused of Seven Cases of Murder and Three Cases of
    Attempted Murder 138

    The Trial and Sentencing 139

    Doubts Emerge 140

Reopening of the Case 142

Justice Miscarried 143

CHAPTER 5: The Richardson Murders in Canada 145

The Discovery of the Crime Scene 145

A Shocking Suspect 146

Steinke Goes on Trial 147

A Lethal Romance 150

The Aftermath 151

CHAPTER 6: The Good Hart Murders 153

Family on Vacation 153

A Horrific Crime Scene 154

Evidence and Theories 155

The Suspects 157

Joseph R. Scolaro – Embezzler? 162

Nothing Resolved….Yet 165

CHAPTER 7: Beslanowitch – The Murder of a Teen Prostitute 166

The Life of Krystal Beslanowitch 166

Cold on the River Bank 167

Reopening of the Case 168

DNA Points the Finger 169

Simpson's History – It Wasn't His First Murder 170

Chapter 8: Murder or Accident? 172

Sherri Miller and Pam Jackson Disappear 172

    A False Accusation 174

    Skeletons in the Studebaker.................................... 176

CHAPTER 9: When Suicide is Murder 178

    The Death of Pamela Shelly...................................... 178

    Television Steps In 181

    Ronnie Hendrick... 182

CHAPTER 10: Snatched From the Snow 184

    The Disappearance of Maria Ridulph....................... 184

    A Tragic Discovery... 186

    Prime Suspect Right From the Start – Was Tessier Johnny? 187

    A Mother's Deathbed Confession 188

    A Long-Awaited Trial... 190

CHAPTER 11: Captive for 24 Years – the Joseph Fritzl Case .. 191

    An Incestuous Situation 191

    A Visit to the Hospital Invokes Suspicion 193

    The Trial of Josef Fritzl 194

    The Psychological Scars and Fighting Back to Normality .. 194

CHAPTER 12: A Controversial Case of Police Misconduct – Or Was it Murder By Cop? 196

    Nizah Morris Left Lying in the Street...................... 196

    Police Request a Second Opinion............................ 197

    The Investigation into the Officers......................... 199

    Police Advisory Commission Called In.................... 199

Something Good from Something Bad 200

TRUE CRIME STORIES VOLUME 3 201

Introduction 203

CHAPTER 1: The Melaniee Road Murder Case 205

    A Good Girl 206

    A Vicious Attack 206

    The Case Goes Cold 208

    A Circuitous DNA Match 209

    The Trial and Unanswered Questions 211

CHAPTER 2: The Keddie Cabin Murders 213

    The Horror in Cabin 28 214

    The Sharp Family 214

    What is Known about the Crime 216

The Investigation 219

    A Rogues' Gallery of Suspects 221

    The Keddie Cabin Murders Today 226

CHAPTER 3: Joseph "The Axe Man" Ntshongwana 228

    The Axe Man 229

    From Rags to Riches 229

    Stalking His Victims 230

    A Bizarre Trial and New Revelations 232

CHAPTER 4: The Disappearance and Murder of Ryan Lane .. 234

    The Disappearance 235

    A Plan Gone Awry? 238

    The Evidence 239

CHAPTER 5: The Torture and Murder of Junko Furuta 242

    The Abduction 243

    An Adult Crime but Juvenile Time 246

    The Aftermath 248

CHAPTER 6: Christian Dornier's Rural French Massacre 250

    Christian Dornier 251

    The Massacre 254

    Insanity Defense 257

CHAPTER 7: The Mysterious Murder of Jessica Lynn Keen ... 261

    A Good Girl Gone Bad 261

    Jessica's Murder 263

    Modern Science Reveals the Killer 264

CHAPTER 8: Mattias Flink's Swedish Shooting Spree 267

    Mattias Flink 269

    Washing Falun in Blood 271

    Life In and Out of Prison 272

CHAPTER 9: Matthew Tvrdon's White Van Rampage 276

    The Death Van 276

    The Sentence 279

CHAPTER 10: The Case of the Real Life Zombie, Tyree Smith 282

Eyeballs Taste Like Oysters 283

CHAPTER 11: The Cold Murder Case of Wilhelmina and Ed Maurin 287

A Brutal Murder 288

Two Suspects Emerge 289

CHAPTER 12: The 1993 Long Island Railway Shooting Rampage 294

Colin Ferguson's Early Life 295

The Transition to a Race Warrior 297

Colin Ferguson's Race War 299

A Most Bizarre Trial 300

The Aftermath of the Shooting 302

Conclusion 304

More books by Jack Rosewood 306
Get These Books for Free 310
A Note From The Author 311

TRUE CRIME STORIES

12 Shocking True Crime
Murder Cases

True Crime Anthology Vol.1

By
Jack Rosewood

INTRODUCTION

In the annals of criminal history, most cases are open and shut. A crime takes place, the police investigate, an arrest is made, and the accused is either acquitted or convicted of said crime. Some criminal cases make for interesting prime time specials or cable network documentaries, but few invoke mysteries that persist for any length of time.

But some crimes are so puzzling and perplexing that the mystery surrounding them takes on a life of its own. It is these mysterious crimes that often have the greatest impact on all involved.

Crime in general has profound effects on the victims specifically and the greater society in general. Murders, in particular, leave behind gaping psychological wounds that often only begin to heal when the perpetrator is caught and convicted for his/her crimes.

But what happens when the murderer is never identified? Or worse yet, what happens when the victim is never found, as if the person vanished into thin air?

These are the type of crimes that tear at the social fabric of a community more than any other – crimes where a suspect is never identified, a body is never found, or a reason for the crime is never determined.

The world is full of many mysteries and within the pages of this book you will be introduced to twelve of the most intriguing and amazing mysteries in modern criminal history. Some of the cases here involve multiple crimes where coincidences seem to link what are otherwise unrelated cases. Investigation of these cases reveals that sometimes although events may be creepy, they are in fact coincidences; while in other cases the jury is still out.

A number of high-profile disappearances are also given consideration in the following pages. While a mysterious fog of uncertainty still hangs over one of these cases, excellent police work and modern science helped locate other missing individuals.

Finally, this e-book considers a number of unsolved murder cases that were all but forgotten about and went "cold," only to heat up and get resolved years, even decades, later through advances in science and new eyewitness testimony.

The world is truly and amazing place full of many mysteries, which includes the criminal world as you will see in this intriguing and exciting e-book.

CHAPTER 1:

A KILLER COINCIDENCE? THE MARY MORRIS MURDERS

In the 1984 science fiction classic *The Terminator*, a murderous cyborg from the future played by Arnold Schwarzenegger, hunted women in Los Angeles named Sarah Connor in order to stop a woman with that same name from giving birth to a man who would kill the cyborg's masters in the future. The plot was totally outlandish and not meant to portray or emulate any real event or situation, but a pair of murders in Houston, Texas in 2000 shocked area residents and to sci-fi fans it appeared to be a case of reality imitating art.

In the span of less than one week, two women both named Mary Morris were murdered in eerily similar ways in Houston. Once the local media made the connections between the two women's names, then other connections were quickly made: the two women looked alike, the manner of their murders was similar, and their bodies were discovered in similar locations. With that many similarities most people were convinced that the murders were somehow connected.

Was a serial killer using the *Terminator* as an inspiration for his sick homicidal fantasies?

The residents of Houston were on edge in the late months of

2000. Anyone could be the killer, and any woman named Mary Morris could be the next victim!

Mary Henderson Morris

Mary Henderson Morris was a forty-eight-year-old wife and mother who worked hard as a loan officer at Chase Bank in Houston. She and her husband had built a good life for themselves and lived in the reasonably affluent Houston neighborhood of Spring Valley. They were hardworking, successful people who were well liked by the neighbors, friends, and family. By all accounts, the couple had a good relationship and neither was involved in drugs or criminal activity, which makes this part of the case the most puzzling.

The morning of October 12, 2000, began as any other in the Morris household. Mary woke up first, got ready for work, and left the house about six am. But Mary never made it to work.

Mary's husband of five years, Jay, usually spoke with her several times during the day on the phone, so he began to worry when the afternoon came and he had yet to hear from his wife. Mary's daughter from a previous marriage, Marilyn Blalock, and Jay filed a missing person report early that evening about the same time a burned car was discovered in a vacant field.

A call was made to the Harris County Sheriff's Department at about 10 am that morning about what was believed to be burning debris or leaves. Later in the day, police arrived at the wooded area to find that it was not debris or leaves that were burning, but an automobile. After the fire was put out the sheriff's department determined that a charred female body was inside. It was the body of Mary Henderson Morris.

The fire made it impossible for coroners to determine the method of death, although it was quickly ruled a homicide. A search revealed that Morris' purse and wedding ring were missing, which suggested robbery, but too many questions remained.

If it were a robbery, why was her car not taken? Why would a robber, or robbers, go to such lengths to conceal part of their crime?

The crime was obviously not a carjacking because the car was burned. Even if it were an attempted carjacking gone bad, there would have been no reason to take the car and its owner to a remote location, kill the owner, and then burn the car.

And why was the car dumped and burned in a vacant lot?

The more investigators looked at the case, the less it made sense.

There were also no witnesses to her abduction or murder.

Due to the circumstances, authorities quickly determined that this was no ordinary murder case, but little did they know how extraordinary the case would become.

Just four days later, after the Morris family put Mary to rest on October 16, Blaylock made the painful, yet seemingly simple journey to the coroner's office to retrieve some of her mother's personal effects.

Instead she walked into an episode from the *Twilight Zone*.

"They told me they still had Mary Morris' body," recalled Blaylock. "I was freaking out. I was thinking we just had the funeral. I saw the remains, and I was looking at something that wasn't even my mother."

It turns out that the woman Marilyn Blaylock saw on the coroner's table was not her mother, but was in fact another woman named Mary Morris—Mary McGinnis Morris!

Mary McGinnis Morris

In many ways other than just the name, Mary McGinnis Morris shared a number of similarities with Mary Henderson Morris, which makes this case all that more eerie. Although Mary McGinnis was a bit younger than Mary Henderson at thirty-nine years old, both women were attractive, gregarious brunettes. Mary McGinnis was also a professional woman who shared a nice suburban home with her husband.

On October 16, 2000, the Harris County Sheriff's Department found the body of Mary McGinnis Morris badly beaten with a single gunshot to her head in a location about twenty-five miles from where Mary Henderson Morris was found days earlier.

Mary McGinnis was also found murdered in her car in a vacant lot in Harris County. Although the vacant lots were located on different ends of the county, both spots had an eerie familiarity.

In life and death, the two women shared some uncanny similarities, which raised the obvious question—who would want to kill the two Marys?

Suspects and Theories

Although authorities were at a loss trying to find suspects and reasons for the murder of Mary Henderson Morris, they quickly zeroed in on two potential perps for the Mary McGinnis case.

At the time of her death, Mary McGinnis worked as a nurse

practitioner and medical director at Union Carbide in Houston. Her supervisors noted that she was a good employee who got along with all of her co-workers and likewise almost all of her co-workers liked Mary, with the exception of one—Duane Young.

Duane Young was a nurse who worked alongside Mary, and as their time working together progressed, he apparently became obsessed with her. Young's obsession with Mary began innocently enough; he hung around her desk at work and engaged her in conversation whenever he could. The behavior at first seemed to Mary McGinnis to be more of a "puppy love" type situation than that of an obsessed maniac, but eventually Young's façade of a "lost puppy dog" was lifted to reveal the stalker that he was. As Young's menacing looks and comments towards Mary reached a creepy crescendo, she found the words "death to her" scrawled on her desk calendar. After numerous complaints to her bosses about Young's inappropriate and borderline illegal behavior, which was verified by co-workers, the stalker nurse was fired on October 13, just two days before Mary disappeared. The note scrawled on Mary's desk proved to be the last straw.

Weeks before her disappearance and death, Mary McGinnis bought a handgun that she kept hidden in her car. Owning a gun in the United States, especially in the state of Texas, is no big deal, and some even consider it not just a right, but an obligation. Mary McGinnis, though, was never a hunter or gun enthusiast, so when she started packing a pistol, her closest friends and family members knew that she was frightened of something or someone. Although Mary was a bit of a private person, she apparently felt that the threats from Young, or perhaps someone else, were grave enough that she needed to be armed because she did tell a couple of her closest friends about the handgun. Mary was no expert in firearms, so her husband gave her the gun and showed her how to use it.

Also, the day Young was fired Mary's employers told her to stay home in order to defuse the situation, which turned into a scene anyway, as Young demanded to see Mary and had to be escorted out of the premises.

October 15th was the last day Mary was seen alive.

By all accounts it was another Sunday for Mary McGinnis; she ran a number of errands and visited a friend named Laurie Gemmell. According to Gemmell, McGinnis called her from a store during the afternoon to tell her, "There is someone here who is giving me the creeps." Not long after that call, McGinnis then called 911.

The transcript of the 911 call has never been released to the public, but a detective who worked on the case and heard the tape said that it, "had their blood chilled listening to it."

After the 911 call, Mary McGinnis' trail went cold.

When Mary did not return home that evening, her husband of seventeen years, Mike, filled a missing person report. In an unfortunate twist that brought Mary McGinnis' case together with Mary Henderson's, the body of McGinnis was found shot to death in a vacant lot outside of Houston.

Despite the similarities of both women being found murdered in their cars, the method of murder was clear in the McGinnis case—she had died of a single gunshot to the head from her own gun.

At first glance, it looked like a suicide, but as homicide investigators examined the scene more closely, they learned that the scene looked staged and it was instead a poor attempt to throw them off. Mary had been beaten and gagged, and her car keys were left outside the car.

Investigators quickly learned about Duane Young, who then went to the top of their suspect list. But as homicide detectives looked into Young's background, Mike Morris soon joined Young as a person of interest.

Morris supplied investigators with samples of his DNA and gave initial interviews, but he declined to take a polygraph exam, hired an attorney, and refused to cooperate with investigators as the case dragged on. Morris also refused to allow his sixteen year old daughter to be interviewed by police. Since it is a person's constitutional right not to talk to police in the United States, Morris did nothing legally wrong in that respect, although his actions placed him further under the police radar.

The more investigators focused on Morris, the more they learned that there was trouble in paradise at the Morris household. Although it was never proved, allegations of infidelity by both Mike and Mary surfaced. Infidelity is always considered as a motive in spousal murder. Whether it is murder to get rid of a spouse in order to be with a paramour, or done out of anger towards a cheating spouse, unfaithfulness must always be considered motive by police. The infidelity motive seemed to go nowhere but it was not long before more perplexing inconsistencies came to light.

It was learned that Mike had taken out a $500,000 life insurance policy on Mary, which alone is not enough to convict or even get someone arrested for murder, but greed is one of the most common motivations for murder throughout history.

Then there was the mysterious phone call.

Records indicate that on the afternoon of October 15th, about two hours after she called 911, Mary received a call on her cell phone from Mike. Mike claims that he did in fact make the call when he was with his daughter at a movie, but that the call went straight to voice mail. Records show that the call was answered and lasted for four minutes. Morris claimed that the phone company must have made a mistake! Although it is possible that the phone company could have made a mistake, it seemed extremely convenient for the suspect in a murder investigation that such a mistake, which is nearly unheard of, would happen at this critical juncture.

Mary McGinnis was also not robbed. In fact, the only valuable item that appeared to have been taken from her was a ring, which was later found in the possession of their daughter. Mike later told investigators that his wife had lost the ring before her murder and that he and his daughter had found it in the house later.

The final piece of circumstantial evidence that points towards Mike Morris as the perpetrator in his wife's murder is the actual murder weapon. The gun that was used to kill Mary McGinnis was actually Mike's gun. He gave the gun to Mary after Duane Young's stalking reached its peak, and only he and some of Mary's closest friends even knew about the gun or where she hid it underneath the seat.

Clearly, many of Mary's friends, law enforcement, and the people of Houston in general began to think Mike was good for his wife's murder, but the evidence was just not there to make an arrest, never mind win a conviction in front of a jury.

Eventually, Mike and his daughter moved back to his native West Virginia where he still presumably lives to this day.

But even if Mike Morris or Duane Young was responsible for the murder of Mary McGinnis Morris, the elephant in the room remains: was her murder connected to Mary Henderson Morris'?

A Hit Gone Wrong?

Once the theory of a homicidal cyborg from the future that came to Houston to kill women named Mary Morris was eliminated, investigators were left trying to determine if the two crimes were connected or just some strange, macabre coincidence. It is difficult to get past the two victims similar names, appearance, the type of location where the bodies were discovered, the manner in which they were killed.

Because of the plethora of similarities, many have concluded that either Mike Morris or Duane Young hired a hitman to kill Mary McGinnis, but in a cruel case of mistaken identity also killed Mary Henderson.

An anonymous caller to the *Houston Chronicle* said: "They got the wrong Mary Morris," in reference to the murder of Mary Henderson Morris.

But investigators remain unconvinced that the two homicides are related.

"As far as the dates go, they are so close they could be linked," said Harris County sheriff's detective Wayne Kuhlman. "But when someone is hired to kill someone, they are going to have their information and know their habits. Hit men don't just go out with nothing."

As of 2016 both cases remain cold.

Sometimes reality is stranger than fiction.

CHAPTER 2:

THE DISAPPEARANCES OF THE PALMER BROTHERS

It seems that in the world today one is never far from another person. In the decades just before World War II, the most industrialized nations witnessed a rapid migration of their populations from rural to urban and suburban areas. Because of that trend, most of us have to travel a distance to truly get away from the noise of civilization. Even denizens of rural areas are usually not very far from their closest neighbors and only a short drive to the nearest town or city. In areas that are more remote, such as the American west, freeways, trains, and airplanes connect formerly isolated areas to the rest of the world.

The American state of Alaska may be an exception to this rule.

Alaska, the United States' forty-ninth state, is aptly named the "Last Frontier" because of its vast expanses of territory that has rarely, if ever, been walked on by human feet. The size of Alaska is immense; it is comprised of 663,268 square miles of land, which makes it by far the largest American state and larger than all but twenty of the independent nation-states of the world.

In contrast to Alaska's vast size, its population is relatively modest. With only 710,231 inhabitants, Alaska ranks forty seventh out of fifty American states in population and nearly half of those reside in the Anchorage metropolitan area.

Alaska's vastness has become somewhat of a pop culture phenomenon in recent years, with a number of television shows being produced there, such as *Tougher in Alaska*, that chronicle the harshness of the Alaska frontier. The book and movie *Into the Wild*, based on the true life adventures of Christopher McCandless, also depicted the beauty and range of the Alaskan frontier while also showing its potentially dangerous side.

If there is anywhere in the industrialized world where one can get lost, it is Alaska!

In fact, in the United States, Alaska has the dubious distinction of having the most missing persons per capita, more than twice the national average.

People disappear into the Alaskan wilderness every year and some, such as Christopher McCandless, even do so willingly, which at first glance makes the next case seem like just another missing person file from Alaska; but further examination of the Palmer brothers' disappearances reveals another set of bizarre coincidences that are stranger than fiction.

A Family of Men

The Palmer family seemed to be made for life in Alaska. A family of men, the siblings included oldest brother Chris, middle brother Charles "Chuckie", youngest brother Michael, and sister Hannah. The three boys and their sister grew up together in Wasilla, Alaska, which has become famous in recent years for being the home of former Alaska governor and vice presidential candidate, Sarah Palin. The three Palmer brothers enjoyed spending time with each other and engaging in typical Alaskan activities including hiking, fishing, hunting, and snowmobiling. They enjoyed the rugged frontier lifestyle of Alaska and all it has to offer.

Life in Alaska was good for the Palmer family, until things took a bizarre and tragic turn on June 3, 1999.

The Disappearance of Michael

Fifteen-year-old Michael Palmer was enjoying his summer vacation from school the same way many American boys his age do—hanging out with his friends and pushing the boundaries of his parents and the law. On that night, he slept over at a friend's house, and after his friend's parents went to bed the crew snuck out of the house to see what kind of trouble they could get into.

Michael and his friends went to a few different parties that night and engaged in some drinking, although his friends would later say that none of them, including Michael, were too drunk to navigate their bicycles. The group spent their time at the parties drinking some beer, visiting with friends who they had not seen since the end of the school year, and trying to make time with girls. At one party, a fight broke out that Michael was involved in, but he was not believed to be the reason for the fight, and like everything else during the night, it was not considered out of the ordinary—just some tough Alaska boys blowing off some steam.

After a couple hours of party hopping, the boys decided to ride their bikes back to the home of the boy they were supposed to be staying the night with. Although the nine-mile ride was fairly long, Michael and his friends were all in good shape and used to such long treks across the vast Alaskan outdoors. The boys rode in single file with Michael taking up the rear, but when they arrived at the house, Michael was nowhere to be seen.

Michael Palmer had vanished into thin air!

The boys later told authorities that they thought Michael had changed his mind and decided to ride home to sleep in his own bed, so they did not report him missing until later the next day. Once Michael was reported missing, the local authorities and the Palmer family began their search in earnest.

Local police quickly found Michael's bike in a river, but were quick to state that they did not believe he drowned. The boy was athletic and knew how to swim, the river was fairly shallow, and a log jam down river would have caught his body if he did in fact drown.

The next major clue was even more puzzling. Michael's shoes were found wet and neatly placed side-by-side next to an airstrip about 200 yards from the river. No airplane had taken off the night of the boy's disappearance and the neat placement of the shoes suggests that Michael placed them there. They were not strewn about as if there had been a struggle.

But some started to believe that Michael was the victim of violence that began at one of the parties he attended on June 3. The police interviewed and gave polygraph examinations to everyone who was known to have been at the parties, with special attention given to boys involved in the fight that was mentioned earlier. Everyone passed their polygraph exams.

It should be noted that people often "beat" polygraph exams, but those who do are usually adults who are often seasoned criminals, not high school boys who got into a fist fight. Besides, how many teenagers can keep a secret? It seems that if one of Michael's classmates had something to do with his disappearance then someone would have said something by now.

But the disappearance of Michael Palmer quickly grew as cold as an Alaskan winter.

The Disappearance of Chucky Palmer

Perhaps the worst part of losing a loved one to a disappearance is the unknown. For years the Palmer family wondered what had happened to Michael. Was he abducted and murdered? Did he become disorientated and wander deep into the forest where he died? The disappearance of Michael Palmer faded from the memory of the people of Wasilla but was never totally forgotten. Conspiracy theories based on no credible evidence began to circulate, and before too long Michael's disappearance became legendary in that part of Alaska. But to the Palmer family, the loss of their youngest brother was never legendary; it was the source of constant pain and a void that could not be filled.

As the years passed by, the other Palmer children became adults and started families of their own. They never forgot about Michael, but the pain of losing him diminished somewhat, and the family finally looked to be moving on. The siblings remained close in adulthood, especially brothers Charles "Chucky" Jr. and Chris, taking part in many typical Alaskan adventures in the outdoors.

But the thought of what happened to their youngest brother was never far from their minds.

"Two brothers aren't supposed to go missing from the same family," is what oldest brother Chris said when the seemingly impossible happened – his brother Chucky vanished into thin air in much the same circumstances as Michael.

On April 10, 2010, nearly eleven years after Michael disappeared, Chucky, Chris, and some of their friends went on a snowmobile trip on Bald Mountain, about an hour outside of Wasilla. April in Alaska is still cold enough to support winter sports; but spring is usually right around the corner, so the most hardcore Alaskans often like to get one last skiing, snowmobiling, or ice fishing trip in during that month.

In the morning, it seemed to the Palmer brothers that they had picked a good day for their end of the season snowmobile trip. The weather was nice, and there was plenty of snow left on the mountain for the men to make plenty of trails, but before the men even got started, signs pointed towards an impending tragedy. Oldest brother Chris, who was a much more experience snowmobiler than Chucky, had to stay behind because the handlebars on his snowmobile snapped. Not wanting to miss out on possibly the last chance of the season to snowmobile, Chucky continued on with his friends. Interestingly though, Chucky, who was admittedly the weakest snowmobiler in the group, brought up the rear of the convoy much like his brother Michael did with his friends eleven years earlier.

Unfortunately for the Palmer family the result was the same!

Chucky, like Michael, disappeared into thin air. As soon as Chucky's friends noticed that the thirty-one-year-old was missing, they retraced their tracks and searched Bald Mountain for their friend. As minutes turned into hours, the situation became more desperate, and professional search teams from Alaska Mountain Rescue were called in to find the missing Palmer brother. Snow and low visibility hampered the search teams, but once the snow stopped searchers located Chucky's snowmobile.

Chucky's snowmobile was found off the main path in a drift with no footprints nearby. Many people think that the lack of footprints is the most eerie aspect of the case, but there is no reason why there would be any since Bald Mountain was the recipient of over two feet of snow at the time.

The search continued after the snow melted, but no body or further clues were ever discovered on Bald Mountain. It was as if the mountain just swallowed Chucky whole.

With Chucky's mountain disappearance, the remaining Palmer family and the entire world for that matter, is left wondering how this is possible and what are the chances? Even if foul play were responsible for the disappearance of one or both of the Palmer brothers, the chances of that happening twice in the same family must be extremely small. Most people could never imagine such a thing happening once in their family, never mind twice.

Perhaps Chris Palmer best summoned up his family's tragedies in layman's terms: "I never thought I'd have to deal with this shit ever again."

The world will probably never know what happened to the Palmer brothers, but they are proof that lightning can strike twice!

CHAPTER 3:

THE LIQUID MATTHEW CASE

Some of you reading this may have been to a dinner party theater production, which have become popular over the last several years. If you have not been to one of these productions, the concept is interesting: as the diners enjoy a meal, a play takes place that usually involves some type of murder mystery. The audience/diners are often encouraged to get involved by offering their clues and/or theories concerning the crime.

In the end, the caper is solved, the cast takes a bow, and everyone goes home full and satisfied with an interesting night out.

Several of you have also probably taken part in a scavenger hunt at some point in your lives. Some of the most elaborate scavenger hunts take place over several miles of territory and sometimes, like dinner party theater, involve a fictional crime that has taken place. In order to solve the fictional crime you have to locate a clue, which then leads you to the next clue in another part of town and so on and so forth. The clues are often written as cryptic poems that, to those not involved in the game, would seem very bizarre and creepy.

For those of you who have been a part of a dinner party theater or a crime based scavenger hunt, you probably have fond memories of the event.

But what if your scavenger hunt somehow miraculously became part of a real murder investigation?

That is exactly what happened in suburban Miami on December 6, 1983. The case became known as the "Liquid Matthew Case" because of cryptic writings that were found at the scene of an apparent homicide.

A Body and Cryptic Clues

On the morning of December 6, 1983, residents of the quiet Miami suburb of Hialeah, Florida awoke to the grim display of what appeared to be a corpse on the side of a road. Local police were quickly called to scene and after searching the body, determined that the male had fallen victim to murder. The body showed signs of strangulation, but little more than that could be determined. The victim had no identification on him, and area residents did not know who the man was. At first, the police could only say that the man was a Hispanic John Doe.

Homicide detectives cordoned off the area and began their search for the usual forensic evidence—a murder weapon, footprints, or even a blood trail.

But the evidence they found proved to be truly unsettling, even for veteran detectives.

Taped to a nearby sign, investigators noticed a bag, and within that bag was a handwritten note that said, "Now the motive is clear and the victim is too. You've got all the answers. Just follow the clues."

At first, the investigators believed the note was some type of prank. What else would explain the cryptic note being found at the scene? After all, only in *Batman* movies do criminals leave riddles at the scene for law enforcement to solve. In fact, some police officers on the scene thought that it may be the work of some sort of scavenger hunt, although that would not explain the dead body laying just feet away. But when they found another note taped to the back of a nearby speed limit sign, they began to fear a psychotic killer was on the loose in suburban Miami.

"Yes, Matthew is dead, but his body not felt. Those brains were not Matt's because his body did melt. For Billy threw Matthew in some hot boiling oil. To confuse the police for the mystery they did toil," read the contents of the second note.

The police were confused and confounded with the cryptic message. What did it mean? Was Matthew the name of the Hispanic John Doe? Was a man named Billy his killer?

As the authorities struggled to find answers in the bizarre murder mystery, which became known as the "Liquid Matthew Case," the public became extremely frightened when the details emerged. The residents of sleepy Hialeah were just as confused as the police and afraid that a thrill killer or serial killer was operating on their streets.

Residents of the community began to barricade their homes and arm themselves for a potential showdown with a serial killer, and the local police began working overtime to solve the enigmatic crime.

But the investigation soon turned up a benign explanation for the notes.

The Explanation

As the police investigation into the Liquid Matthew Case progressed and its details were made public, it was learned that the notes were actually part of a Halloween murder mystery game/scavenger hunt sponsored by four area churches. It turns out that the notes and the game fell victim to the rainy south Florida climate. After the game was completed, organizers failed to pick up all of the notes because heavy rains that swamped the Miami area.

As for the victim?

Police eventually identified "Liquid Matthew" as a Columbian sailor named Francisco Patino Gutierrez. It is believed that Gutierrez was probably killed in one of the many drug smuggling schemes that were prevalent in Miami during the 1980s, but the details remain unknown.

With that said, local authorities can say unequivocally that Gutierrez's murder and the cryptic scavenger hunt notes were not connected in any way. He was not boiled to death and whatever his killer, or killers, name was, it was clear that the person had no intention of even remotely identifying himself.

The Liquid Matthew Case was just one big bizarre coincidence.

CHAPTER 4:

THE BRIGHTON TRUNK MURDERS

The "Queen of Watering Places"

The city of Brighton, United Kingdom, often known colloquially as "Brighton Beach", has been one of the prime destinations for the British for over 200 years. Brighton boasts of some of the nicest beaches in Britain, relatively warmer temperatures compared to the rest of the country, and a plethora of bars, nightclubs and concert venues. Because of these things, Brighton has earned the nickname the "Queen of Watering Places."

Besides being a top vacation destination, Brighton has also been known as a safe, peaceful city. Outside of a spate of counter-culture youth violence during the 1960s and '70s—which was made known to the world through the rock band The Who's 1973 album *Quadrophenia* and a 1979 film of the same name, as well as the popular Stray Cat's song "Rumble in Brighton"—and the Irish Republican Army bombing of a hotel in 1984, crime in Brighton has been historically low.

Therefore, Brighton's idyllic setting makes this next case, or series of cases, especially interesting.

During the course of just over 100 years, Brighton was the scene of three bizarre, similar yet unrelated murders. Another murder that took place in London shared many of the hallmarks of the other three murders and was also determined to be unrelated. Collectively, these four murders are known as the "Brighton Trunk Murders."

Due to their mysterious and bizarre circumstances, any one of the trunk murders could probably be given its own entry in this anthology. When considered as a group, due to the coincidence factor, the Brighton Trunk Murders are probably the strangest case examined in this book.

The 1831 Murder

In 1831, Brighton was in the middle of one of its early boom periods. Tea, spices, and gold were flowing into England from its lucrative colonies in India and South Africa, which resulted in a trickle-down effect of wealth whereby the middle class was growing at a phenomenal rate. The result was good for Brighton, as members of the growing middle class were able to travel to the beachfront community on new rail lines and spend their disposable income in the city's bars and shops. Life was good in Brighton, and most of its inhabitants were happy.

Celia Holloway was an exceptional woman for her time; she was a painter on the chain pier who was not reliant on her husband John. She spent her days painting the ocean, beaches, and anyone who passed by. Celia was a happy, independent woman who lived in a time when it was not common for women to have those views or lifestyle. The progressive-minded Brighton seemed to be the perfect place for her to pursue her interests while she was happily married to John.

But sometimes things are not as they seem.

Apparently, John was not happy being married to a liberated woman, so he murdered her, placed her body in a trunk, and then buried the trunk under Lover's Walk. John Holloway was quickly arrested for his wife's murder, convicted, and hanged all within a year. Justice was quick in nineteenth century Britain.

So began the long, bizarre saga of the Brighton Trunk Murders.

Minnie Bonati

Although the next murder in the series of Brighton Trunk Murders took place in London, which is about fifty miles from the sea resort city, the circumstances of the crime are eerily similar enough to the others that it warrants being included in this macabre list. On May 7, 1927, an attendant at the Charing Cross train station in London became concerned with a foul smell emanating from the luggage room. Upon investigating the odor, he soon learned that source was a luggage trunk. Correctly believing that he may have stumbled onto a crime, the local police were called to investigate.

The police discovered a grisly scene—a dismembered body with each piece wrapped in paper. Also included in the trunk were several items of clothing, including a pair of underwear marked "P. Holt."

The circumstances of the discovery shocked and frightened Londoners when it became public. The average Londoner at the time was a street-smart person and no stranger to crime. Theft, prostitution, and even murder were all crimes that Londoners were used to hearing about in 1927, but this was quite different. Most of the murders that took place in London at the time were cases of criminals preying on each other, personal and/or financial grudges, or of someone ending up in the wrong part of town. Murders with this level of brutality were almost unheard—almost.

It was less than fifty years earlier, in 1888, when five women were raped and murdered in London's east end in the "Jack the Ripper" murders. In 1927, when the dismembered body was found in the train station, some of the older residents of London were reminded of the Jack the Ripper case and wondered if there might be some connection.

But the London Police quickly dismissed any such outlandish claims as they quietly pieced together the identity of the victim.

After a thorough investigation, police learned that the woman to whom the underwear belonged was still alive, but that one of her former employees, thirty-six-year-old Minnie Rolls/Bonati, could not be located. Fearing that the case would go cold, investigators went public with the details and soon a taxi driver came forward who said that he gave a ride to a man with a large trunk in tow to the Charing Cross station on May 6.

Police eventually identified the man as thirty-six-year-old real estate agent John Robinson. Under pressure during police questioning, Robinson eventually admitted to the murder and dismemberment stating: "I met her at Victoria and took her to my office. I want to tell you all about it. I done it and cut her up." Robinson claimed self-defense to the police. He said that after he brought Bonati back to his office, for some reason she attacked him, so he defended himself with a coal shovel, hitting her in the head with a fatal blow. He then dismembered her body in the office, placed it in a trunk, and called for a taxi to take him to the train station.

Perhaps he believed that since Bonati was a prostitute no one would care and he could get away with the murder, but the dismemberment was much too much for the civilized nature of early twentieth century London.

The mountain of physical evidence, along with his confession, was too much for Robinson to overcome in trial. He was quickly convicted and executed on August 12, 1927, just over two months after the murder.

The "Girl with the Pretty Feet"

By 1934, the luster of Brighton beach had worn off a bit as the United Kingdom, along with most of the industrialized world, was in the midst of the Great Depression. The crowds that had flocked to Brighton's beaches dwindled as the average British citizen found saving what little money he had more important than a weekend at the beach. To most people at the time, the Great Depression seemed to have made Brighton's golden age a thing of the distant past, which was further exacerbated by a series of macabre events that began in June of that year.

On June 17, an unclaimed trunk at Brighton train station was noticed by an employee. The employee, William Vinnicombe, was not alarmed so much by the trunk being left at the station, but more so by the foul odor coming from it. Perhaps aware of the 1927 murder of Minnie Bonati, Vinnicombe called local police to investigate the trunk's contents.

Chief inspector Ronald Donaldson quickly learned that like the Bonati case, he was staring at the dismembered corpse of a woman!

In fact, the trunk only contained the woman's torso, head, and arms; the legs were recovered in a suitcase the next day at another train station.

Unlike the Bonati case, there were few clues to the dead woman's identity tucked into the trunk. A piece of paper with the word, or name, "Ford" was found in the trunk, but it was never determined if it was connected to victim, if it was a "red herring", or possibly some random paper that ended up in the trunk. A coroner's examination determined that the woman was around twenty-five years old and pregnant. A cause of death was never determined. The manner of death could have been an accident, but the brutal dismemberment of the body clearly pointed towards homicide. The Jane Doe quickly became known as "the girl with the pretty feet" because her feet were believed to be those of a dancer's.

But someone would notice if a dancer was missing—at least that is what investigators believed. Unfortunately for the girl with the pretty feet, no one came forward on her behalf, which led many to believe that the victim was a prostitute.

Going on the prostitute theory, investigators scoured brothels and red light districts and began to focus on a family doctor who often performed illegal abortions on the side, often for prostitutes. The suspect was a man named Edward Massiah, who lived in the neighboring town of Hove.

Although Donaldson suspected Massiah, the medical examiner who performed Jane Doe's autopsy was not so sure, as he noted that the dismemberment did not appear to be the work of a professional.

Massiah was also apparently well connected with local police and politicians.

Donaldson's superiors forced him to back off of his investigation of Massiah, who then quietly moved to London where he continued to practice medicine, both legally and illegally. Any doubts concerning Massiah's influential connections were put to rest when a woman whom he performed an abortion on died, but he was never charged.

Massiah retired to the Caribbean in the 1950s and the case of the girl with the pretty feet was never solved.

As strange as the case of the girl with the pretty feet was, it was made even stranger when it was revealed that another trunk murder case was taking place in Brighton at the same time!

The Murder of Violette Kay/Saunders

Forty-two-year-old Violette Kay and Minnie Bonati shared some dubious distinctions—they were both prostitutes who were both murdered, dismembered, and then shoved into a trunk. It is doubtful if either Kay or Bonati ever saw herself working as a prostitute and there is no possible way that either could have foreseen the awful circumstances in which their lives ended.

Violette Kaye, also known as Violette Saunders, worked as a prostitute in the Brighton area and dated a twenty-six-year-old man known as Toni Mancini, although his legal name was Cecil England. For legitimate work, Mancini worked as a bartender and bouncer at local bars, but his true passion was in the world of crime. He was known to the local police as a low level player in the local criminal underworld—a thug who the heavier players could employ to do dirty work.

Although Mancini worked as a bouncer and occasional heavy for underworld figures, the majority of his violence was reserved for those closest to him. He was known to slap his girlfriends around in front of others if they did not do as he pleased, but Violette Kaye was a bit different than his other girlfriends. Kaye was known to stand up to Mancini's threats and violence and would even fight back.

Kaye and Mancini's relationship was volatile to say the least.

The fact that Kaye was nearly twenty years older than her paramour contributed to the turbulent nature of their relationship, as she was lacking in self-esteem and jealous to the point of violence. Kaye and Mancini frequently drank copious amounts of alcohol, which then turned their drinking sessions into shouting matches and sometimes fisticuffs. It was during one of these drinking sessions that Violette Kaye was seen alive for the last time.

On the night of May 10, Kaye and Mancini were drinking heavily at Mancini's place of employment, the Skylark Café. As the drinking binge progressed, Kaye accused Mancini of having an affair with a young female employee at the bar named Elizabeth Attrell. Questions by Kaye turned into loud accusations as she began to become more intoxicated, and before she and Mancini left for the evening, the two were witnessed shoving each other.

That was the last time anyone saw Violette Kaye alive.

In the days after May 10, Mancini acted extremely suspicious, giving some of Kaye's personal effects to Attrell and telling Violette's friends and family that she had suddenly moved to Paris. Kaye's sister then received a telegram that claimed to be from her sister in Paris, but it was later revealed that the message was in fact sent from Brighton.

Mancini then took up residence in an apartment near the Brighton train station, in the days after the dismembered body of the girl with the pretty feet was discovered.

As the local police searched the area around the train station for clues to murder of the Jane Doe, they eventually conducted a house to house search, which led them to the apartment of Toni Mancini. Once inside Mancini's apartment, they were quickly overwhelmed with the smell of decay.

They found the body of Violette Kaye stuffed into a trunk at the foot of Mancini's bed!

The public was surprised at the eerie turn of events. How could there be two extremely brutal, yet similar, murders committed at the same time in the quiet vacation resort town of Brighton?

Certainly Toni Mancini must be the killer of both women, right?

The police quickly determined that Mancini was not the perpetrator of the Jane Doe murder; it was just simply another bizarre coincidence in the series of "trunk murders" as they became known. They were confident, however, that Mancini killed Kaye in act of anger on the night of May 10. An autopsy, which was conducted by the same doctor who examined the remains of the girl with the pretty feet, concluded that Kaye died from a blow to the head.

Mancini went to trial for Kaye's murder in late 1934, which the prosecution believed would be an open and shut case. The fact that Kaye's rotting corpse was discovered in Mancini's apartment was thought to be damning evidence alone, but for good measure the prosecution paraded a litany of witnesses who all testified to the defendant's seedy nature. Former and current girlfriends, one who testified that Mancini tried to get her to give him a false alibi to the police, and criminal associates all gave proof, in the prosecution's eyes, that Mancini was the type of person who would murder his girlfriend.

But the strategy backfired.

The defense acknowledged that their client had a criminal background, which is why he attempted to hide Kaye's body *after* he found her dead. The defense further argued that the true perpetrator was probably one of Kaye's many "clients" who was still on the streets of Brighton.

The jury agreed with the defense and acquitted Mancini of all charges.

But the bizarre case of the Brighton Trunk Murders does not end there; Mancini admitted on his deathbed in 1976 that he was in fact responsible for Kaye's death, although he claimed it was an act of self-defense.

The Brighton Trunk Murders truly left an enduring psychological impression on the people of the United Kingdom. For a number of years after the Mancini trial, the British quit referring to their beloved beach getaway as the "Queen of Watering Places" and instead called it the "Queen of Slaughter Places."

Today, the memories of the bizarre string of murderous coincidences that took place in and around Brighton are fading into the distant past. Most of the younger generation does not even know about the Brighton Trunk Murders, and the popular resort town has once again claimed its spot as Britain's prime beachfront vacation spot.

That is, until the next body is found in a trunk near the train station.

CHAPTER 5:

THE ABDUCTION AND MURDER OF ANNIE LE

America's Ivy League colleges are known for their strict academic requirements and as factories that produce world leaders in the fields of business, science, and politics. The campuses of Ivy League universities are full of history as the halls are named for famous Americans and their architecture is often centuries old. Truly, Ivy League schools are in a world of their own.

The residential neighborhoods that have grown up around the nation's Ivy League schools are usually pretty safe. For instance, Dartmouth is located in the bucolic setting of New Hampshire and Harvard and Princeton are located in low crime suburbs of major cities. Columbia is located in Manhattan, but since the 1990s the crime rate has been very low in that city.

Yale University is a different story.

Yale University, like its Ivy League brothers, is an incredibly fine academic institution that has graduated a number of brilliant minds from around the world; but it is also located in the middle of New Haven, Connecticut.

Since the Puritans first arrived there in the seventeenth century, New Haven has attracted several waves of immigrants. Irish,

Italian, and Jewish immigrants immigrated there in large numbers during the nineteenth and early twentieth centuries, and then groups from within the United States, such as blacks from the South, and Puerto Ricans, have moved there in the later twentieth century. The immigrants made New Haven a hard-scrabble, blue collar city that has experienced growing pains over the years.

One of the growing pains New Haven has experienced is a high crime rate.

Gang and drug violence has contributed to place New Haven in the top twenty of the most dangerous American cities per capita, where it enjoys the dubious distinction of being grouped with some of America's more notorious cities, such as Detroit, Chicago, and Memphis. New Haven's high crime rate has been a source of problems for Yale University for a number of years and made national headlines when Yale graduate student Annie Le mysteriously vanished from an on-campus laboratory on September 8, 2009.

A Woman with a Promising Future

In September, 2009, Annie Le was a woman with an incredible future in front of her. At twenty-four years old, Le was a doctoral student of pharmacology who was engaged to be married on September 13. She enjoyed being a student at Yale and was well liked by her friends and colleagues. Le was looking forward to marrying her fiancé Jonathan Widawsky and beginning her life in "the real world."

The petite Le was a highly ambitious young woman who grew up in the San Jose, California area. Le was from a traditional, yet

Americanized Vietnamese-American family that placed a high value on education and family, which she dutifully followed in her own life.

From an early age Le showed a keen interest in science and medicine. She volunteered in her community, studied hard, and was always there for family members. Eventually, her hard work paid off, as she graduated as the valedictorian of her high school class and was accepted to the University of Rochester where she earned a BA in bioscience in 2007.

The bright and ambitious Le was then accepted into the pharmacology graduate program at Yale where she was studying enzymes in order to develop treatments for diabetes and cancer.

But all of the hopes and dreams of this bright young woman were needlessly dashed in a bizarre crime that became the focus of national attention.

The Crime

Despite being located in the middle of a high crime city, Yale University is equipped with several levels of security. University police regularly patrol the campus looking for any student in need of help and investigating anything that may seem out of the ordinary. Property crimes have been high at Yale compared to other campuses in the state of Connecticut, but violent assaults and homicides are almost unheard of, which is no doubt at least partially the result of campus police patrols.

Yale University also has other security measures in place to protect its students and staff.

A number of close circuit television cameras strategically placed around the campus record the movements of people in and out of the campus buildings, and many of the buildings can only be accessed with a current Yale University identification card.

Both of the last two security measures played an important role in the Annie Le case.

The morning of September 8 began just as any other for Annie Le. She woke up, had breakfast in her apartment, and then took public transportation to Sterling Hall on Yale's campus where she had an office. She left her purse, phone, and other valuables in her Sterling Hall office and then went to conduct research at the on-campus laboratory around 10 a.m.

Cameras in the laboratory captured images of her entering the building, but not of her leaving.

Le usually returned home in the afternoon, so when she failed to come back to the apartment, her roommate reported her missing around 9 p.m..

Campus, local, and state police, along with the FBI, immediately locked down the campus laboratory and began an exhaustive search for Le. It appeared that one of Yale's brightest stars had been abducted from campus.

The case immediately attracted media attention. A bright, attractive Ivy League student had disappeared from campus with no trace. Le's anguished family and her fiancé appealed to the public for help in press conferences, but as the country watched and hoped for the safe return of the graduate student, some doubted the circumstances.

Some people began to question if she was really abducted and began to propose that maybe she willingly chose to disappear.

Perhaps the stress of her rigorous studies combined with doubt about her impending marriage made Le become a runaway bride. Those closest to Le dismissed such theories by pointing out that she only showed hope and excitement for her future and never displayed any signs of doubt towards her marriage. There was no way that Annie Le would have ruined her future and hurt family and friends in such a way, they said. Unfortunately, on September 13, the day of Annie Le's planned wedding, the thoughts of her family and friends were confirmed — the young graduate student's body was discovered in a basement wall of the laboratory.

The Killer

An examination of Le's partially decomposed body revealed that the young woman had been strangled to death and was sexual assaulted. Initially, authorities cast a wide net in their potential suspect pool, which included friends, co-workers, and acquaintances of Le's, but once her body was discovered in the basement of the lab they knew that the killer was someone she worked with.

On the afternoon of September 10, before Le's body was discovered, graduate student Rachel Roth, who also worked in the lab, noticed what appeared to be a blood smear on a box of towels. Roth alerted authorities to the find, and while she waited for police to arrive she noticed twenty-six-year-old lab technician Raymond Clark acting strangely. She said he repositioned the box of towels so that the apparent blood smear was not visible and then cleaned a drain that did not appear to need cleaning.

Clark then told Yale police that he talked to Le in the lab on

September 8, but that she left the building just after noon.

The video surveillance clearly showed that Le never left the building, and Raymond quickly became a person of interest in her disappearance. The police also noticed some scratches on Clark's face, but he claimed that he received the injuries from a cat.

Although arrows of suspicion began to clearly point towards Clark early in the investigation, authorities still did not know if they had an abduction, homicide, or runaway bride on their hands.

Further investigation of the laboratory turned up a discarded lab coat that was stained with what was later determined to be blood, some bloody clothing, and work boots with Clark's initials.

Le's body was eventually discovered when the odor from decomposition became apparent to investigators, who then brought in cadaver dogs that located her corpse. Authorities obtained a warrant for Clark's hair, blood, and fingernails on September 15th, which was then matched to some of the items discovered in the lab and on Le's body. The lab technician was arrested on September 17th when he then failed a polygraph examination, which proved to be the final nail in his homicidal coffin.

After a series of pre-trail motions, at the urging of his parents Clark pleaded guilty to Le's murder in March, 2011. The judge sentenced Clark to forty-four years in prison with his release date in the year 2053.

If Clark survives natural causes and the clutches of hardened career criminals, he will be seventy years old when he is released.

Unanswered Questions

The abduction and murder of Annie Le is both a tragic and bizarre tale on so many levels. The tragic nature of the case is obvious: a bright young woman who had so much to offer the world was viciously murdered before her life had a chance to get underway.

The case was bizarre from start to finish.

Her apparent abduction from the supposed safe confines of an Ivy League science lab to the revelation that she was murdered and "hid" inside the lab were all details that make sure this case will never be forgotten.

But perhaps the most mysterious aspect of the case revolves around the killer, particularly what drove Clark to kill Le.

At his sentencing, Clark appeared genuinely contrite as he fought back tears and made a statement to the court.

'Annie was and will always be a wonderful person, by far a better person than I will ever be in my life. I'm sorry I lied. I'm sorry I ruined lives. And I'm sorry for taking Annie Le's life,' said Clark at sentencing.

Despite showing remorse for the horrific act, Clark never told the court why he killed Le.

Raymond Clark was a lab technician who did not get along well with the graduate students and scientists that worked in the lab, as some described him as a "control freak." One lab researcher said that Clark would get upset if others did not follow the smallest rules of the lab, such as wearing shoe covers. "He would make a big deal of it, instead of just requesting that they wear them," said one of the scientists.

Some believe that Clark, a man with limited education who was little more than the laboratory's janitor, felt extremely inadequate around the graduate students and scientists and therefore would make a major issue about minor problems in order to exert some power. On the day he killed Le, Clark sent her a text message requesting a meeting to discuss the sanitary conditions of the cages of the mice that were used for experiments.

Did Le meet with Clark and say something that set the man off into a murderous rage?

If that is the case, there is little in his past to suggest such a thing, and the two worked together for about four months with no signs of turmoil or acrimony. Friends of Clark's were all quick to point out that they were extremely shocked when they learned he murdered Le.

"This is not the Raymond Clark that I know," said Clark's childhood friend Maurice Perry. "I've known him so long. I just can't picture him doing something like this."

Neighbors also described Clark, who lived with his girlfriend and a dog, as thoughtful and considerate.

Yale University president Richard Levin also showed surprise, although his statement was no doubt to at least partially cover himself and the university from a law-suit by Le's family. Levin stated: "His supervisor reports that nothing in the history of his employment at the university gave an indication that his involvement in such a crime might be possible."

Unfortunately, Raymond Clark proved that when it comes to murder, anyone is capable and anything is possible.

An Eerie Footnote

We all know that words we say, if not chosen correctly, can have a tendency to come back to haunt us, but in Annie Le's case, words she *wrote* continue in many ways to haunt Yale's administration.

In February 2009, just months before she was murdered, Annie Le wrote a short article in Yale Medical School's *B Magazine* titled: "Crime and Safety in New Haven." Le's article focused on what Yale students can do to protect themselves from the crime in New Haven.

She wrote: "In short, New Haven is a city, and all cities have their perils, but with a little street smarts, one can avoid becoming another statistic."

Unfortunately for Annie, no amount of street smarts could help her avoid the peril in the laboratory that ultimately made her a statistic.

CHAPTER 6:

THE DISAPPEARANCE OF THE MCSTAY FAMILY

As detailed in this book, disappearances are not that uncommon and some, such as the vanishing of the Palmer brothers, are downright creepy. No matter how bizarre some missing person cases are, most tend to involve just one person. Whether the person involved got too intoxicated and wandered off, succumbed to the effects of Alzheimer's disease, or was the victim of a homicide, the vast majority of disappearances only involve one person.

Logic and statistics dictate that the chance of more than one person disappearing at the same time from the same place is extremely low. For instance, if a group of people wander from their camp into the wilderness, the chances are pretty good that either one of the campers will be found by a search party or one of the group will make his way back to the camp. The same goes for an abduction-homicide; it is extremely difficult to abduct and murder multiple people at the same time, even if there are multiple killers involved.

These facts are what make the 2010 disappearance of the McStay family in Fallbrook, California both peculiar and frightening.

By all accounts, the McStay family—which was comprised of forty-year-old father Joseph, forty-three-year-old mother Summer, four-year-old boy Gianni, and his three- year-old brother Joe Junior—were an average American family. They lived a relatively comfortable life in a quiet suburban neighborhood that was paid for with the profits from Joe's contracting business and Summer's work as a real estate agent.

The McStays never mentioned to family or friends that they were taking a trip, and they were not known to have any enemies, which is what made their sudden disappearance frightening and the subject of nationwide media attention.

The Disappearance

Joe and Summer never indicated to their friends and family that anything was wrong in their household or that the family was planning on taking any extended trips. In fact, the family had just celebrated Joe Junior's third birthday on January 31, and by all accounts the family appeared happy and content, which made their sudden disappearance all the more mysterious.

After repeated calls from Joe's brother Mike went unanswered, Mike entered the home through a window on February 15 to investigate. The family dogs were in the backyard unfed and there were signs that the family left quickly because food was left out. Mike then called local police to report the strange circumstances and officially begin a missing persons investigation.

The initial police investigation turned up a number of clues, but they only added more mystery to an increasingly enigmatic case.

Although the left out food and the unfed dogs indicated that the

McStays left their home in a hurry, there were no signs of a struggle. With the help of Mike and other family members, the police were also able to ascertain that nothing valuable was missing, so a scenario of a home invasion/burglary was quickly ruled out.

The Fallbrook police and San Diego Sheriff's Department quickly canvassed the neighborhood and interviewed all of the McStay's family, friends, and neighbors, which then resulted in a couple of more important clues.

A neighbor's security camera caught images of a car leaving the McStay residence at 7:47 p.m., but the car did not belong to either Joe or Summer! Unfortunately, although technology has come a long way, the resolution of the camera was not good enough to identify the image/s of anyone in the car or the car's license plate. For the time being the mysterious nighttime visitor to the McStay home was a dead end, but it possibly fit part of a bigger picture that had yet to be painted.

The police next interviewed Joe's friend and business partner, Chase Merritt, who said that he received a call from him at 8:28 p.m.. Merritt let the call go to voice mail, as he claimed he often did, because if it was important or work-related then Joe would leave a message.

Joe did not leave a message.

The next major break in the case came on February 8, when the family's Izuzu Trooper was found in the San Ysidro neighborhood of San Diego, which is just north of the international border of the United States and Mexico. The discovery of the McStays' family car was thought to be a big lead, but ultimately raised more questions than there were answers.

Did the McStays simply go to Mexico for a vacation? If so, why did they not tell any of their family or friends? Why did they leave their beloved pets in such a sorry condition? And perhaps the most important question: why would they go to Mexico in the first place?

Tijuana, which is the major Mexican city just south of the border, is a popular destination for many Americans, but it would not be a stretch to say that the city is not exactly family friendly. Tijuana is more known for its brothels, strip clubs, and availability of drugs—both legal and illicit—than it is for any family attractions. Tijuana is clearly not a place where most people would bring two young children.

And why would the family leave their car and walk into Mexico?

There seems to be no reason why they would have done this. Some people argued that perhaps the entire family was trying to get "lost" and moved south of the border to do so, but it no doubt would have been easier to do so with the family car, at least for a while. They could have always sold the car at a later time.

The location of the car on the border raised more questions than there were answers, and many of the McStays' family and friends began to believe that the car was staged at the border by other people, possibly for nefarious reasons.

As family and friends began to doubt that the McStays were in Mexico, police uncovered another clue that once more turned the investigation upside down. A forensic search of the family's computer revealed that on January 28, internet searches were made about travel in Mexico, specifically what type of documentation children would need to enter the country.

Perhaps the McStays, for whatever reason, simply had enough of life in America and decided to leave on a whim to Mexico. After all, Summer and Joe were known to be free spirits, so maybe the situation was not so nefarious.

Or maybe they had to leave town quickly for more ominous reasons.

The McStays' family and friends remained unconvinced that Joe and Summer would have taken their children to another country without telling anyone, but without more evidence there was little that the police could do.

The disappearance of the McStay family would remain one of the most highly reported missing persons cases in recent American history.

Media Attention and Investigation

As the clues and circumstances of the disappearance of the McStay family emerged, the situation became one made for the media. Images of the attractive couple and their cute little boys were repeatedly flashed across television screens, newspaper articles, and webpages.

The case quickly came to the attention of one-man crime crusader John Walsh, who hosted the popular weekly show *America's Most Wanted*. Walsh's show profiled notorious criminals who were on the run, as well as missing children, which Walsh often became emotional about since his own son was abducted and murdered by a serial killer in 1981. The McStay family disappearance seemed tailor-made for *America's Most Wanted*, so the case was profiled on a June 2010 episode. A number of viewers called into the tip line after the episode aired, but unfortunately they all turned out to be dead ends.

The McStay case was also featured on the similarly themed show, *Unsolved Mysteries,* hosted by late actor Dennis Farina, but again, the tips that were generated led nowhere.

As the months that the McStay family was missing turned into years, the police, John Walsh, and Dennis Farina were not the only people investigating their disappearance; former radio talk show host and author Rick Baker also threw his hat into the ring.

Baker began investigating the case independently from the police shortly after the family went missing. He interviewed friends, family, and potential witnesses and came to some interesting conclusions in his book, *No Goodbyes: The Mysterious Disappearance of the McStay Family.* Baker's interest in the case began when he interviewed Mike McStay on his San Diego radio show in 2011. After the radio interview with McStay, Baker compiled a list of potential sightings of the family and followed up on them, which took the radio host throughout Latin America.

Four days after the McStays vanished, a video of a family of four crossing the U.S.-Mexican border on foot surfaced, but it could not be determined who they were. After that report, more and more tips of sightings in countries such as the Dominican Republic, Belize, and Haiti kept a glimmer of hope alive for the friends and family of the McStays.

Baker packed his suitcases and went to a number of the exotic locales to follow up on the leads. "I've traveled around the world to what I thought were verified sightings," said Baker, but ultimately none of them panned out.

The supposed Latin American connection led many to believe that violent drug cartels may have been responsible for the family's abduction, even though there were no signs that either of the parents owed drug debts. There was also no evidence that apart from some occasional marijuana use either of the McStay parents ever took "harder" drugs such as cocaine, methamphetamines, or heroin. Joe and Summer McStay just did not fit the profile of drug cartel victims.

The location of the McStay's Izuzu also did not seem like the work of a drug cartel to Baker. "Why did they stage the car? A cartel is not interested in staging anything," said Baker.

Baker's observation is correct in regards to cartel activities south of the border, but it is commonly known that the cartels keep more of a low profile in the United States and refrain from some of their more blatant acts of extreme violence. With that said, it does seem like a lot of effort for gang members to go through to somehow cover up the abduction of a middle class American family.

As Baker's independent investigation continued, the police began to focus on a suspect who was right under their noses.

A Suspect Emerges

Charles "Chase" Merritt, now fifty-nine years old, was a friend and occasional business associate of Joe. The two men worked on a number of projects in the area installing fountains, which was Joe's specialty, and were generally known to get along well.

Decorative water fountains that are often seen in the yards and driveways of expensive homes are what Joe specialized in and how he was able to provide for his family. Business slowed during 2008 and 2009, as it did for the entire construction industry nationwide, but at the time of the McStay family disappearance business was picking back up. Joe was finally able to start saving some money again for his family, and he was also able to hire more employees and give some work to his friends such as Charles Merritt.

Although Merritt and McStay did not spend too much time together outside of work—after all, Joe had a family to look after—by all accounts they got along fairly well and considered each other colleagues and friends. Also, a large part of Merritt's income was derived from work McStay sent his way, so at first glance it seemed unlikely that he would have anything to do with Joe and his family's disappearance.

But Merritt was the last known person to see Joe.

Merritt told police that he met Joe at a Chick-fil-A restaurant in the afternoon to discuss some potential future contracts and receive payment for some completed jobs. He claimed that McStay seemed fine and that the two left and went their separate ways after the brief meeting. As the last person to see Joe McStay, a certain amount of suspicion was cast Merritt's way, but that alone is not enough to arrest someone for a crime, which is if a crime in fact took place.

But it turns out that Merritt also had a bit of a shady past.

Merritt was a convicted felon who had a rap sheet that included burglary and possession of stolen property. His last conviction came in 2001. Although Merritt had a criminal record, all of his convictions were for non-violent offenses and no one that knew him indicated that he was capable of abducting four people. He was not known as a violent person and had no known altercations with Joe.

The case into the disappearance of the McStay family continued to go off into several directions, and as time went by media interest began to wane. Many in the McStay family began to question if they would ever know what happened to their loved ones.

Then on November 13, 2013, the case took an unfortunate turn.

The Discovery

San Bernardino County in southern California is the largest county in land mass in the United States. Although the county is also quite populated, with over two million inhabitants, most of those people live in towns such as San Bernardino, which are just outside of Los Angeles County in the far western end of the county. Once you get east of San Bernardino, the county is a vast sea of desert and mountains that stretches all the way to the state lines of Nevada and Arizona.

It is exactly the type of place where a person can easily go missing, alive or dead.

On November 13, a motorcyclist discovered the remains of the entire McStay family in two shallow graves outside of the town of Victorville. The search for the McStays was finally over, but the case then evolved into a homicide investigation.

Although the bodies had apparently been in the ground since the time of their disappearance, the dry desert climate preserved the bodies of the adults quite well. An autopsy determined that the parents, and more than likely the children as well, were killed by blunt force trauma to the head, although the bodies of the children were too degraded to tell for sure. A sledge hammer recovered from one of the graves was probably the murder weapon.

Charles Merritt was arrested the next day for the family's murder and in pre-trial hearings it was revealed that the police had amassed a mountain of evidence on him during their investigation.

Much of the evidence against Merritt is circumstantial, but it is voluminous and appears quite damning.

The investigation into Merritt's background discovered that the contractor with a modest income liked to spend several days at a time in the area casinos.

And Merritt was not winning!

To pay for his gambling losses, Merritt wrote over $21,000 in checks on Joe McStay's business account and then cancelled McStay's QuickBooks accounting membership on February 8, 2010, the day the McStay's Izuzu was discovered near the international border.

The circumstantial evidence against Merritt further piled up when it was discovered that he withdrew thousands more from Joe's business account during the period from February 9, 2010, well into March, to pay for extended trips to area casinos.

Merritt's DNA was also recovered from the family's Izuzu, which can certainly be argued away as he was an associate's of Joes, but when taken with the other evidence, looks to be the final straw in the camel's back of circumstantial evidence.

Merritt now sits in the San Bernardino County jail and faces the death penalty if he is convicted. Perhaps in an effort to stall the inevitable, Merritt has fired five different attorneys, which has caused considerable delay to the trial. Although the surviving members of the McStay family are glad that an arrest has been made, the loss of their loved ones will always weigh heavy on their hearts.

Although it looks like all arrows point towards Charles Merritt as the killer, some doubt if he is the sole perpetrator. One argument is that it would be too difficult for one person to kill four people, even if two of them were children. The reality is that Joe trusted his business associate and he therefore never saw him coming, so to speak. Once the McStay parents knew what was happening, they probably complied in order to save their children and by the time they got to the desert outside Victorville, it was too late.

In a case as strange as the McStay family disappearance, conspiracy theories are bound to take hold, and even if Merritt is convicted and put to death, some will continue to doubt that all the facts have come to light.

The true tragedy of the McStay murder case is that they were murdered by someone they trusted who killed them for the oldest motive known to man—greed.

CHAPTER 7:

THE RAYNA RISON MURDER

In recent years, cold cases that were solved through advances in science have been featured on popular documentary television shows such as *Forensic Files* and *The New Detectives*. These shows stress the unbiased nature of DNA in contrast to the often un-credible accounts of witnesses. The reality is that many criminals are smart enough to leave no traces of physical evidence. Crafty criminals often wear gloves to conceal their fingerprints and destroy the bodies of murder victims in order to destroy any physical evidence that could point towards their guilt. Bodies are also often moved from the scene of the murder to another location by the murderer in efforts to confuse homicide investigators. And sometimes criminals just get lucky and no physical evidence is left at the crime scene, or what little was, has been degraded by the time forensic investigators find it.

Because of the sometimes crafty nature of killers, oftentimes investigators are forced to rely upon the age old evidence of eye-witness testimony. The problem with eye witnesses is that humans can be notoriously unreliable at times. People might be scared to offer testimony, or they may feel some sort of misplaced loyalty toward a criminal.

But sometimes, if given enough time, circumstances and a guilty conscience will lead to unknown or once thought unreliable witnesses to help solve a murder.

This is what happened in the 1993 murder case of Rayna Rison.

A Promising Future

Located about an hour's drive east of Chicago on Interstate 80, LaPorte County, Indiana, is known for its low crime, affordable housing, and generally being a good place to live. The people of LaPorte County take pride in their homes and schools and are known for being friendly, helpful people.

Sixteen-year-old Rayna Rison was one of LaPorte's friendly inhabitants.

Rayna enjoyed spending time with her parents, Bernie and Karen, and she was particularly close to her sister Wendy, who was one year her junior. Rayna excelled in school and was known to be a popular girl who got along with most of the disparate cliques that are often found in American high schools.

In her spare time, Rayna worked part-time at the Pine Lake animal clinic in the town of LaPorte. The veterinarians she worked for stated she had a natural gift for the position and would no doubt someday realize her dream of becoming a veterinarian and opening her own clinic.

But that dream was shattered when she vanished from the animal clinic on the night of March 26, 1993.

When Rayna failed to come home that night her parents and sister began to worry. The responsible sixteen-year-old always checked in with her parents, especially if she stayed all night at a friend's. Rayna's parents called around to her friends, but no one had seen her.

It was if she had vanished into thin air.

The local police and sheriff's department soon got involved, and the search for Rayna Rison became a missing person case.

The Search for Rayna

Friends and family of Rayna joined together with local law enforcement to find her by searching local ponds, rivers, and fields. Her family also plastered the area with flyers that had recent pictures of Rayna. The extensive search quickly paid off when Rayna's car was located a day after her disappearance in a rural area of LaPorte County, but there were no signs of Rayna.

An examination of Rayna's car seemed to reveal nothing that could help investigators: there was no blood present, and there was no damage to the car. It was as if she simply drove the car to that location and then left it for whatever reason. The discovery of the car raised a lot of red flags, but the local police were quick to point out that at that point they only had a missing person case on their hands.

The disappearance frightened residents of LaPorte County and also brought media attention to the area.

Rayna's disappearance was featured three times by John Walsh on *America's Most Wanted* in just one month, and Oakland Athletics owner and part time LaPorte resident, Charlie Finley, offered a $25,000 reward for Rayna's safe return.

To some outside LaPorte County, Finley's interest in the case appeared to be grandstanding, but the locals knew he was sincere. Yes, the billionaire had a tendency to be flamboyant at times—one of his best known accomplishments was bringing the rock band The Beatles to Kansas City during their limited American tour in 1964—but he also had a legitimate love for LaPorte County. Finley donated much of his money to support schools in the county and even lived in the area while he owned the Athletics. But despite the immense media attention, profiles on *America's Most Wanted*, and the reward offered from Finley's own pockets, the police received no credible leads as to Rayna's whereabouts.

Then, about a month after her car was discovered, the body of Rayna Rison was found in a lake in LaPorte County.

The investigation then shifted from that of a missing person case to a homicide, but unfortunately for the authorities, the fact that Rayna's body was submerged in water for so long meant that it would be more difficult to lift forensic evidence from the scene or Rayna's body.

The autopsy determined that Rayna died of strangulation, and although DNA profiling was becoming more widely used by law enforcement in 1993, no forensic evidence was taken from her body. Police could not even say for sure if she was killed at the location where she was discovered or dumped at the scene. There were also *apparently* no eye witnesses to the murder.

Who would kill such an innocent girl?

The Case Goes Cold

As time moved further away from the discovery of Rayna's body, her murder began to slowly fade from the public eye. Her family held vigils every year and her case had an occasional mention on *America's Most Wanted*, but by 1998 it seemed as though the killer would never be caught.

But then an arrest was made.

Rayna's brother-in-law Ray McCarty, who was twenty-eight at the time of her murder, was arrested and charged with the killing in 1998.

Lori McCarty, who was married to Ray, was Rayna's older sister, and although there was a considerable age difference between the two, the younger sister often spent a lot of time around the McCarty house. Rayna also became close with Ray—too close.

When Ray was twenty-four, he began molesting twelve-year-old Rayna, which resulted in a pregnancy when the girl was just thirteen. McCarty used the typical method of operation of a child predator by first appearing as a friend to Rayna and then using a combination of compliments and threats to sexually molest her. He was eventually convicted of molesting Rayna, served time in jail, and was then placed on probation. The local police were particularly interested in the fact that McCarty threatened Rayna and her parents' lives if she ever revealed the truth of his despicable acts.

She did report him and was later murdered.

Almost immediately, McCarty was the top suspect. Besides his past crimes and threats against Rayna, he was unable to account for his whereabouts during the time Rayna was abducted. Despite the circumstantial evidence against McCarty, there was no physical evidence and no eye-witness that could place him with Rayna the day she disappeared.

Perhaps feeling a bit of pressure, the LaPorte county prosecutor's office charged McCarty with murder in 1998, but released him fifteen months later when it was clear there was not enough evidence to convict him.

Investigators either had to find more evidence against McCarty or look for new suspects.

Was Rayna the victim of a local serial killer?

Larry Dewayne Hall was described by many as polite and mild mannered, yet beneath the calm exterior lurked a raging serial killer. Larry Hall was a native of Wabash, Indiana, who worked as a janitor and enjoyed taking part in Civil War reenactments in his free time.

He also enjoyed killing women.

Hall confessed to killing a number of women, and some authorities believe the count may be as high as forty. They think that as he traveled the country taking part in battle reenactments, he was also killing women. So far, Hall has not garnered as much attention as other more well-known serial killers, but that may change if more murders are definitively attributed to him.

In 2010, a book written by Christopher Martin titled *Urges: A Chronicle of Serial Killer Larry Hall* was published that argued Hall may be Rison's killer. He pointed out that Hall and McCarty knew each other in grade school, which suggested that there may have been collusion in Rayna's murder. Martin also stated that a police search of Hall's home turned up a box of birth control pills with Rayna Rison's name on it, although investigators said that none of the drug stores in the area had a prescription for Rison.

He was also apparently out of the area doing a reenactment when Rayna disappeared.

It was never explained why Hall had those pills in his possession, but some investigators believe it was part of one of the killer's sick fantasies. Hall, like many other people in Indiana, simply followed Rayna's case and got some sort of perverse pleasure out of fantasizing about the details of her death. LaPorte County authorities were adamant that there was no way Hall was Rison's killer.

To the public, it seemed as though Rayna's killer, or killers, may never be caught. But behind the scenes, as Martin was attempting to finger Hall, the police were about to nab the killer.

Old Loyalties are Shattered

The criminal underworld is an interesting place. Yes, there is a criminal code where it is a big no-no to be a "snitch" or informant for the police, but it is also a society where every man is out for himself; loyalties are often tenuous and subject to change depending on the situation a criminal may find himself in, such as the capricious nature of his cohorts. A criminal who is tight-lipped and loyal to another person at one time may find that loyalty detrimental to his own life in the future.

The criminal underworld is also a domain driven by fear.

Some of the most successful criminals keep their underlings under control through extreme acts of violence that are perpetrated either on others for the underlings to see, or on the underlings themselves. A criminal is less inclined to give the police information on one of his associates if the person is known to employ extreme violence against his enemies.

In the cold case murder of Rayna Rison, the crime was ultimately solved not through forensic evidence, but by the police breaking through the warped sense of loyalty and violence that pervades the criminal underworld.

Thirty-eight-year old Jason Tibbs was arrested in August 2013 for the murder of Rayna Rison. The arrest came as a surprise to many in LaPorte County who expected her killer to be an outsider like Dewayne Hall, but it turns out that he was in fact at the top of the suspect list at the beginning of the investigation.

At the time of Rayna's disappearance and murder, Tibbs was eighteen and had briefly dated Rison. It was quickly determined that Tibbs still held a flame for Rayna as indicated in letters that he wrote to her in which he said he would "go to almost any extreme" to date her again. A ring that was identified as belonging to Tibbs was also found in Rayna's abandoned car.

Also, in the years after Rayna's murder, Tibbs developed a reputation as a violent thug in LaPorte County.

When Rayna's sister and former classmates graduated from high school and went on to start careers and families, Jason Tibbs graduated from the school of hard knocks. Tibbs had encounters with the police throughout the 1990s and was known as a tough guy within the local criminal underworld. A combination of fear and misplaced loyalty helped protect Tibbs from justice for two decades, but time began running out for him in 2008.

Ricky Hammons was fourteen when Rayna Rison was murdered. Like Tibbs, he was a bit of a juvenile delinquent who enjoyed skipping school and smoking pot, and also like Tibbs he immersed himself in the LaPorte County's criminal underworld during the 1990s. In 1999, at the age of twenty, Hammons shot and killed a man in rural LaPorte, which landed him in the Wabash, Indiana, state prison with a forty-five year sentence.

Life had not gone well for Ricky Hammons.

Then in 2008, for reasons that are debated, Hammons reached out to LaPorte County detectives with information in the cold case murder of Rayna Rison. Tibbs' attorneys argued that Hammons made up the information for a reduction to his sentence but LaPorte County prosecutor denied that stating, "There was no deal with a witness despite the suggestion there was."

A man has a lot of time to contemplate his life behind bars.

Perhaps feelings of remorse and sympathy for the Rison family combined with no reason to fear Tibbs anymore made Hammons come forward. It may also be that he just wanted to get even with Tibbs for some reason. Tibbs was known to intimidate and bully younger delinquents in LaPorte County, so maybe Hammons finally saw his chance to get even. Regardless of his reasons, Hammons statements to LaPorte County investigators quickly got the ball rolling that led to Tibbs' arrest.

Hammons told the authorities that on the night of March 26, 1993, he was smoking marijuana in the hayloft of a pole barn when a car pulled in that was driven by his sister's boyfriend, Eric Freeman, with Jason Tibbs along as passenger. He said that Tibbs then opened the trunk of the car where he could see what appeared to be a body wrapped in a blanket. Freeman argued with Tibbs over what happened before Hammons then snuck out of the barn.

Although Hammons' statement appeared to verify what many

LaPorte County investigators originally thought, more evidence was needed to corroborate his story in order to make an arrest. The next step was to locate Eric Freeman.

Locating Eric Freeman was easy, as he too was incarcerated on a murder conviction.

Where it is possible that Ricky Hammons may have been driven by a combination of remorse and sympathy to come forward with information in the murder of Rayna Rison, Eric Freeman was clearly driven by fear, the fear of spending the rest of his life in prison.

Although Freeman is currently serving time in prison for murder, he, like most murderers, will probably be paroled someday. The likelihood of him ever being released would be severely diminished if he was convicted of another murder, so Freeman quickly decided to talk under one condition, that he receive immunity from prosecution for the murder or Rayna Rison.

Unlike in movies and television shows, prosecutors in the real world are usually loathe to award full immunity to criminals in order to obtain their testimony in court. Shaving a few years off an impending sentence is standard, but sometimes full immunity is awarded if the person in question played a significantly lesser role in the crime or there are other mitigating circumstances.

Serving time on a previous murder conviction is clearly a mitigating circumstance since Freeman was going nowhere anytime soon.

Freeman's statement to police and subsequent testimony at Tibbs' murder trial corroborated Hammons' statement and also filled in some important details.

According to Freeman, he rode with Tibbs to the Pine Lake animal clinic so that Tibbs could speak with Rayna and hopefully persuade her to start dating him again. The conversation quickly turned into an argument as Rison was adamant that she did not want to date Tibbs as she was seeing someone else.

Despite Freeman's testimony, the next part of the story remains somewhat enigmatic. For some reason, after she had a heated conversation with Tibbs, Rayna agreed to get into the car with him and Freeman. Freeman then said that he drove the two to a rural area where their argument continued until Tibbs realized he could not win so he then overpowered the girl and strangled her to death. The two men then put Rayna's body in the trunk of the car and drove to the barn to contemplate their next move. It was at this point that Hammons saw Freeman and Tibbs.

After a heated argument over what he had done, Tibbs convinced Freeman to help him dispose of Rayna's body. Freeman claimed he helped Tibbs because he feared going to prison and what the killer might do to him. He also felt a sense of loyalty to his troubled friend. But nearly twenty years later, Freeman feared spending the rest of his life in prison more than his former friend.

On November 7, 2014, primarily due to the testimonies of Hammons and Freeman, Jason Tibbs was found guilty of the murder of Rayna Rison and sentenced to forty years in prison. Under the Indiana Department of Corrections parole system, Tibbs will probably serve just under twenty years.

Despite the length of the saga to bring Rayna's killer to justice and what many believed was too lenient of a sentence for Tibbs, the Rison family has finally found some peace and closure.

"Hopefully now my family can find some semblance of peace from what we've been through for the last twenty years," said Rayna's father, Ben Rison.

CHAPTER 8:

THE MURDER OF SARA LYNN WINESKI

The murder cases that grab the most headlines tend to be ones where the victims are truly "innocent" and in the wrong place and the wrong time. Part of the shock in those types of cases comes from the sense that no matter how safe a neighborhood one may live in, there is always the potential to be the victim of a heinous crime. Indeed, it is relatively rare, even in cities with high crime rates, for people not involved in criminal activity to be murdered.

When people do hear about criminals and people from the lowest rungs of society being murdered, the response is often differential at best. The philosophy holds that the police are here to protect law abiding citizens, not the criminals and other assorted "scum."

But the reality is that the police are here to protect all members of society, no matter what a person's situation currently is. No one is disposable and every life has value, even the lives of criminals and prostitutes.

The best police officers around the world hold this attitude, which was put into action by the St. Petersburg, Florida, Police Department when they discovered the body of forty- nine-year-old prostitute Sara Lynn Wineski.

Around 11 p.m. on May 21, 2005, residents who were staying at the St. Petersburg Ronald McDonald House were awoken up by sounds of screams. Oftentimes in large American cities such sounds go unnoticed, but possibly because of the proximity of the Ronald McDonald House, a resident called the police. The police responded to the scene, but after they saw no signs of an assault or other criminal activity they moved on to other calls.

The next day, the body of Sarah Lynn Wineski was discovered under a deck of the Ronald McDonald House. She had been raped and strangled to death, but other than the ear witness who called into the police the night of the murder, there were no witnesses to the crime.

Police immediately suspected that Wineski, who was homeless and had been working as a prostitute, fell victim to a serial rapist who had been operating in the area. A background check of Wineski revealed that she was new to the Tampa Bay and knew few people, so it was believed that she did not know her killer. Random murders are the toughest to solve, but the St. Petersburg police had one powerful piece of evidence that the killer left behind—his DNA profile.

But the police needed a suspect to link the DNA to, which could take years or might never happen at all.

Sara Lynn Wineski

Sometimes it is easy to write off and forget about crime victims like Sara Wineski. We tend not to give a second thought when crime happens to criminals, the homeless, or those who live "on the other side of town", and when they become victims little is usually said. Sometimes, these people get mentioned in the local press but are often never named. Wineski's killing probably would have been glossed over in the local Tampa Bay press as well, if it were not for the location of her murder. A murder at the Ronald McDonald House, where family members of children undergoing treatment for serious illnesses stay, surely gave unfavorable attention to St. Petersburg.

When she was murdered, Sara Wineski had hit rock bottom. Her life had spiraled out of control through a series of bad relationships, drug use, and criminal activity, but things were not always that way. Wineski was a mother of four and had four grandchildren, and her family still loved her despite her plethora of demons.

"We have wonderful memories of her," said Candice Chessman, one of Wineski's daughters. "And her murderer stole the hope that we all carried in our hearts that we would have the chance to make more memories with her someday."

Wineski had only recently arrived in the Tampa Bay area in an effort to get a fresh start, but with no money or contacts in the area she quickly turned to her old drug habits and prostitution. Prostitution was an easy and quick way for Wineski to make money for her drug habit, although it ultimately was the source of her final demise.

Much of society may have given up on Sara Lynn Wineski, but the St. Petersburg police did not.

A DNA Match

The homicide detectives of the St. Petersburg police department were just as dedicated to catching the killer of Sara Lynn Wineski as any other murderer, and they knew that the small bit of DNA they lifted from Wineski's body would probably be the key to catching him.

Chances are someone who would commit such a terrible crime had either done so before or would again at some point in the future. Despite that grim prospect, it meant that there was a good chance of eventually catching Wineski's killer. The police entered Wineski's killer's DNA sample into the Combined DNA Index System (CODIS) and waited for a match. The CODIS database was established after the DNA Identification Act became law in 1994. CODIS is an FBI program, but samples are taken from all fifty states, the federal government, and the District of Colombia. At first, samples were taken from convicted sex offenders in various states, but over the years the database has grown to include persons convicted of all felonies, and in some states, those even charged with felonies and some misdemeanors. Each individual state determines its own criteria for who is required to give DNA samples, but by 2006 every state had joined the CODIS database on some level.

2006 also happened to be the year when the DNA from Wineski's body was matched to a suspect!

In many ways, the trajectory of Raymond Samuels' life was similar to Wineski's. He suffered from a variety of personal issues, was a drug user, and was homeless and only in the Tampa Bay area for a very short time when Wineski was murdered. But unlike Wineski, Samuels chose to take out his rage on others.

The DNA taken from Wineski's body was definitively matched to Samuels.

It turns out that Samuels was easy to locate. In 2006, he was incarcerated in an Ohio prison with a lengthy sentence for a violent home invasion of an elderly couple. When Samuels entered the Ohio Department of Corrections after his conviction, a sample of his DNA profile was taken and entered into the CODIS database.

Detective Mike Kovacsev of the St. Petersburg police department had not given up on finding Sara Wineski's killer and routinely took the time to enter the DNA of the unknown male taken from the victim into the CODIS database. In late 2006, they matched the sample to Samuels, but waited several more years to charge him.

There were still too many questions that had to be answered before formal charges could be brought, foremost whether Samuels and Wineski knew each other. After all, Wineski was a known prostitute and the DNA sample taken from her body may have been the result of a consensual, paid sexual encounter. Kovacsev and other detectives from St. Petersburg traveled to Ohio to interview Samuels, but the convict asserted his Fifth Amendment right and refused to talk.

Kovacsev was confident that he had his man and kept the Wineski family continually updated about the case.

"The family was understanding," said Kovacsev. "It's not like we had someone out on the street. He was in custody so he wasn't going anywhere."

Forensic technicians ran more tests on the DNA recovered from the scene to make sure they had the right man and, most importantly, they were also able to match DNA taken from a belt believed to be the murder weapon to Samuels.

Samuels was charged with first degree murder in the death of Sara Wineski in 2013 and currently sits in the Pinellas County jail in Florida awaiting trial.

Wineski's family is grateful that Kovacsev and the other detectives from St. Petersburg did not forget about their loved one, despite her past.

"As a family, we are not in denial about where she was in life, but it is important to us that people know that her life was not a waste and not something anyone had the right to take from her," said Candice Chessman. "She was not always homeless and alone."

CHAPTER 9:

THE MURDER OF LITTLE ANNA PALMER

As detailed in the last story, the murder of anyone, no matter his or her background, is always a terrible thing. But the murder of a child clearly brings out a slew of emotions in even the most stoic of people.

What type of person could kill an innocent child? This is a question that psychiatrists, psychologists, and penal experts have attempted to answer now for decades through interviews and examinations of known child killers. Unfortunately, all the studies have apparently failed to unlock the secrets to what makes a child killer tick because the murder of children keeps happening.

With that said, child murder is still a relatively rare phenomenon, and children who follow basic safety rules are usually exempted from the worst category of criminals, which makes the next case all the more frightening.

In 1998, ten-year-old Anna Palmer was like any other kid her age—she liked to spend time with her friends, pets, and family. Most importantly, Anna followed her mother's safety rules, but none of that helped the poor little girl when she was brutally murdered on her family's porch in broad daylight on September 10, 1998.

The Crime

September 10 began just like any other in the Palmer household in Salt Lake City, Utah. At around 5 p.m., Anna called her mother Nancy at work to ask if she could play outside with some neighborhood kids. The Palmer's neighborhood was very safe and everyone knew each other, so it was common for all the kids to meet up and ride bikes or play games like hide and seek. Fifth grader Anna was allowed to take part in the neighborhood activities as long as she told her mother where she was going and came back home at a specific time, usually before dark. Nancy told Anna that it would be fine, but that she should be home by 7 p.m. when she arrived home from work.

When Nancy came home at 7, she was surprised to see Anna lying on the front porch, but when she got closer her surprise turned to horror—little Anna was stiff and in a pool of blood. The petrified mother immediately called 911 and attempted to conduct CPR on Anna, but the poor little girl's throat was gashed and her spinal cord was severed. Anna was dead before Nancy got home.

An autopsy revealed that Anna was beaten and stabbed five times. Either the gash to the throat or the stab to the spinal cord could have killed her. Anna was also sexually assaulted.

After the initial shock of the horrific murder wore off, the mood of the residents of Salt Lake City turned to fear and anger. If such a despicable murder could happen to a girl that seemingly followed all the safety rules and who lived in a safe neighborhood, then no child was safe. The people were also angry, and in the religiously conservative state of Utah, people had biblical retribution on their minds.

The Salt Lake City police had to move fast to catch Anna's killer.

The Investigation

Homicide detectives with the Salt Lake City police department immediately went to work by canvassing Anna's neighborhood and interviewing her friends and family. The case was as bizarre as it was heart wrenching due to the circumstances of little Anna being abducted and murdered all within a matter of minutes, near a busy intersection, and during daylight hours. Despite those facts, no one had seen her taken or murdered.

Or did they?

Detectives quickly put together a timeline for the last two hours of Anna Palmer's life, which helped bring to light a suspect.

After she got off the phone with her mother, Anna walked a few houses down to meet her friend Loxane Konesavanh. The two girls went to a local park and spent most of the next two hours swinging. When it got close to 7 p.m., Anna, being the safe girl who followed her mother's rules, began to walk back home with Loxane. The two girls then noticed that a man was following them, so remembering "stranger danger," they let him pass and said nothing to him. Loxane said that when the man passed them, he turned and glared at Anna.

The two girls then stopped at the yard of fourteen-year-old Amie Johnson to see her new kitten. Loxane then went home a different way than Anna, but Anna was apparently accompanied by the man the two girls had seen before.

"He creeped me out personally," said Johnson, who witnessed the mysterious man walking with Anna. "I looked back and Anna was walking home, and he was still walking behind her like a crazy person. I looked again and no one was there."

Adult neighbors also reported seeing a young man who fit the girls' description lurking around the area earlier in the day. Witnesses said he looked drugged or drunk, but none knew who he was. A man matching the description was also seen walking around the scene of Anna's murder.

Did the killer return to the scene of the crime?

The lead sounded promising to investigators, but identifying the creepy stranger would prove to be extremely difficult. Detectives interviewed everyone who lived in the neighborhood and paid special attention to all known sex offenders. In total, the Salt Lake City Police Department interviewed over 200 people in connection with the murder of Anna Palmer.

Anna's family also got involved by making public appeals via the media for anyone with any information about the little girl's murder to come forward to the police. Further incentive was added with an $11,000 reward for information leading to the killer's arrest and conviction, but still no one came forward. The case quickly became cold.

Although the case may have gone cold, little Anna took an important clue from the killer that ultimately led to his arrest. Despite her size, the little girl ferociously fought her attacker by scratching him, which left some of the killer's DNA profile under her fingernails.

1998 was still early in terms of the CODIS database, but forensic experts with the Salt Lake City police dutifully collected a sample where it would be entered at a later time.

Matt Breck

In 1998, California native Matt Breck was nineteen with no direction in his life. He originally came to Utah with his brother Tom after Tom's friend, Todd Clark, told the two that they could find steady employment and a chance to start over in the Beehive State. Not long after they arrived in Utah, Tom found steady employment, but things did not go that way for Matt.

Clark said Breck thought of himself as a tough guy who would rather spend the day drinking than working. He also said that Breck tried to pick fights with people and liked to carry knives, which he proudly showed to anyone interested. Clark's wife was particularly creeped out by the younger Breck and claims she told a police officer she knew to take a look at Matt when she heard about Anna's murder. Around the time Anna was murdered, Breck was charged with a violent felony in an unrelated case, but had the charged lowered to misdemeanor and served very little time in jail.

Most importantly, no DNA was taken from Breck during his short stay in the county jail.

After he got out of jail in Utah, Breck headed north to Idaho, but instead of getting a new start, his criminal behavior got more extreme. He was convicted of a burglary charge in 1999, served two years, and was released in 2001. Not long after his release, he was picked up on a child molestation charge and given a lengthy prison sentence.

A sample of his DNA was also taken and entered into the CODIS database.

The CODIS system needs to be constantly updated, and agencies that are looking for a match from a DNA sample need to continually check the system—emails are not sent when/if a match is made.

In late 2009, detectives from Salt Lake City finally received the news they were waiting for—a match had been made in the CODIS system to the DNA recovered from under Anna's fingernails. Authorities then went to the Idaho prison where Breck was incarcerated and questioned him about the murder of Anna Palmer. He admitted that he lived in the neighborhood at the time, but denied involvement in her murder or of even knowing the little girl. It was at that point that police knew they had their man.

Breck was then extradited to Salt Lake City and charged with first degree murder and aggravated sex abuse of a child. Utah is a death penalty state and if the death penalty was created for any one person, it would be Matthew Breck. Feeling the anger of the residents of Salt Lake City upon him, Breck took the sensible option and pled guilty to murder in 2011 in order to receive a sentence of life without parole.

Some think that Breck got off easy, but the reality is that as a high-profile child killer, his life in a maximum security prison will not be easy. Breck will be sent to one of Utah's tougher prisons where he will probably have to spend most of his life in a protected wing where he will have few luxuries and only be allowed out of his cell for limited periods. If he decides to enter general population, if he even has that option, where he will be afforded more luxuries and freedoms, he then runs the risk of being beaten, raped, or even murdered by any number of inmates. Child killers are at the bottom of any prison hierarchy, which means that Breck will constantly have to watch his back.

Whether Breck chooses to take his chances in the prison's general population or he checks into protective custody, he most certainly has a miserable life ahead of him.

The tragic and strange case of Anna Palmer's murder could only have been solved through scientific advances, namely the CODIS database. As Sam Gill, the district attorney who prosecuted Breck said: "It was through science that this poor girl, who was tragically and horrifically murdered in our community, was able to basically point to her killer."

CHAPTER 10:

THE STRANGE MURDER OF ROY MCCALEB

One does not have to search the internet very long to find stories of spousal murder. The reasons for spousal murder are varied and diverse—greed, jealousy, infidelity, and anger are some of the more common reasons—but sometimes the motive is not so clear and the circumstances are even murkier.

On September 22, 1985, fifty-year-old Ray McCleb was shot to death as he slept in his Houston home. When police arrived at the scene, it appeared to be a case of a burglary gone wrong, but soon after interviewing Ray's wife, forty-three-year-old Carolyn, investigators realized that they were about to embark on a very strange homicide case.

A Carjacking and a Murder

Houston, Texas, is a large American city with typical American problems, crime being at the top of the list. The violent crime rate in Houston is fairly high, but as with most American cities, one can avoid most of the crime by staying out of certain areas. The McCalebs lived in a middle income neighborhood where crime was relatively rare and violent home invasion murders were unheard of. Still, it was the big city and random crime can happen to anyone.

But once homicide investigators took a statement from Carolyn, they began to see that this was no ordinary murder, and it was probably not random. The account that Carolyn McCaleb gave to the police of her husband's murder was so strange that police initially though that it was too bizarre to make up.

According to Carolyn, she was carjacked and raped by a barefoot man with a knife ten days before her husband was murdered and then, somehow, the rapist learned her address and came back.

On the night Roy was murdered, Carolyn claimed that the rapist came into her room where he tortured and raped her for some time before he found the pistol that she kept under her pillow. The rapist then went into Roy's room, who was heavily sedated from a recent back surgery and also convalescing from a heart attack, and shot him in the head at point blank range in total darkness. The killer then ran for the door when he bumped into Carolyn and dropped the gun, which she then picked up and fired two shots at him, but missed.

Obviously, the story had more holes in it than a slice of Swiss cheese, but the inconsistencies continued to pile up and cast even more suspicion in Carolyn's direction.

The first question that police asked Carolyn was why she did not report the rape and carjacking that supposedly took place ten days prior to her husband's murder. With a straight face and in a calm demeanor, Carolyn simply said that she did not want to upset her husband who was recovering from recent health problems. The answer was suspicious, but suspicion alone is not enough for an arrest, so police began to investigate the carjacker story.

Almost immediately, homicide detectives had a difficult time locating a suspect in the crime because Carolyn's description of the killer was not consistent. In fact, Carolyn said the killer-rapist was white in her first statement, but then later said the assailant was black. When asked how she could get such an important and major detail wrong, she said that being in the south, she was embarrassed and did not want people to think she had an affair with her attacker.

Other details of Carolyn's account of the murder simply did not add up.

Carolyn, Ray, and the supposed killer were not the only people in the McCaleb house that night. Carolyn's son from a previous marriage and his girlfriend were also present when the murder took place. Neither saw an intruder in the home, although both were awake at the time Carolyn claims he made his getaway.

Then there was her behavior after the police arrived.

Carolyn's account was described as rehearsed and for the most part terse. She then took a shower, even though she was explicitly told that doing so would damage any physical evidence from the rape. Although she did go to the hospital after her interview with police, she left before doctors could perform a thorough examination. Finally, she refused to take a polygraph examination.

To most people in the Houston area it appeared that Carolyn was her husband's killer, but despite the circumstantial evidence, Harris County prosecutors were unwilling to charge her without some tangible, physical evidence.

It would be a long time before Ray McCaleb's killer was brought to justice.

The Years Pass By

As the years after Ray McCaleb's murder turned into decades, the case slipped out of the minds of most Houstonians, but the Harris County prosecutors did not forget. Although there was a plethora of physical evidence in this case—they had the murder weapon and the body of the victim—the circumstances prohibited the prosecutors from charging Carolyn. Yes, her story sounded phony, but they had nothing to prove otherwise. But that did not stop the prosecutors from working on the case. A succession of prosecutors continued to quietly keep the case open.

And they were not looking for the mysterious barefoot rapist.

Carolyn was the authorities' only suspect from the beginning, and as they researched the woman's past, they were astonished with what they found!

It turns out that Ray was Carolyn's eighth husband, and she was still legally married to her seventh when Ray was murdered. It turns out that when she left husband number seven for Ray, she took the unlucky guy's $4,000 tax refund check for good measure. The information was enough to get Carolyn charged with bigamy, but was still a long way from homicide.

Further investigation revealed that Ray and Carolyn were only married for a year and a half and that Carolyn was the sole beneficiary of his estate and insurance policy.

Carolyn clearly had a motive to murder Ray.

With the mountain of circumstantial evidence stacked against her, many began to wonder why the bigamist had not been charged with murder. Many people have been charged and convicted with less evidence. What made the woman who became known as Carolyn Krizan-Wilson so special?

It turns out that in the years after Ray's murder, Carolyn inserted herself nicely into the local law enforcement establishment.

Two of Carolyn's sons went on to become officers with the Houston Police Department, and somehow Carolyn was able to land job as a civilian employee with the same department. No doubt Carolyn's connections with the police department were a mark in her favor, but they ultimately did not stop Harris County prosecutors from charging her with murder in 2008.

The charges were big news in the Houston area, and the ensuing court proceedings proved to only add to what was becoming a tabloid television type atmosphere surrounding the case.

Carolyn's attorneys argued that too much time had passed and there was no solid forensic evidence to tie their client to the crime, so the charges should be dropped. In a surprise move to many Houstonians, Judge Kevin Fine agreed and threw the case out of court, but Harris Count prosecutors proved relentless and appealed the decision. A Texas appellate court reinstated the charges in 2012, and word of a plea bargain began to surface shortly thereafter.

In 2013, Carolyn Krizan-Wilson was a shell of her former self. Frail and suffering from Alzheimer's disease at the age of seventy-one, prosecutors came to a deal with Krizan-Wilson's attorneys. Krizan-Wilson agreed to plead guilty to Roy's murder in return for a six-month jail sentence and probation for ten years.

Many thought that Krizan-Wilson should have spent the rest of her days in prison, but prosecutors were quick to point out that in the world we live in today that is obsessed with physical evidence, a hung jury or acquittal was a real possibility. Although some of Ray McCaleb's family did not share that sentiment, others were just glad to see Krizan-Wilson finally admit her guilt.

"She is willingly admitting that she murdered him and that's something we've known all these years," said Ray McCaleb's daughter Pam Nalley. "I think that means more to me than anything."

CHAPTER 11:

ROBERT ZARINSKY – A SERIAL KILLER NABBED BY DNA

There are some people among us who should never walk the streets free. These men, and sometimes women, are career criminals who do untold amounts of damage to society for sometimes long periods of time before they are usually sent to prison, only to be released one day so that they can return to the streets and prey on more victims. For every crime that these predators get caught committing, there are several more that they get away with, often including murder.

Robert Zarinsky was one such career criminal and predator. When he was not incarcerated in a prison, juvenile hall, or a mental hospital, he was on the streets victimizing the people of New Jersey. Eventually, Zarinsky was convicted of murder, but the parole system and sentencing guidelines meant that he could conceivably be released one day to prey on more innocent people. If Zarinsky could prove to a parole board that he was either reformed or no longer a threat to society, then he could be released.

Thanks to modern science, Zarinsky's DNA profile made sure that he would never hurt anyone again.

A Predator from the Beginning

Robert Zarinsky was born in 1940 to a middle class New Jersey family, although the family's income level was about the only thing that was "middle American" about the extremely dysfunctional family.

Robert showed signs of extreme violence and cruelty at a young age that are often the hallmarks of a future serial killer. He was known to torture animals and often beat his sister Judith, to which their mother, Veronica, told her son, "Don't hit her in the face."

Yes, the matriarch of the Zarinsky household doted on and enabled little Robert, which led the future serial killer to commit innumerable anti-social acts. He was never punished for anything he did and was even allowed to victimize his own father. According to those close to the Zarinsky family, Robert routinely dished out physical beatings to the father, Julius, and often took his earnings from the family store that he owned.

Zarinksy clearly received no direction in his childhood, which no doubt contributed to his criminal behavior, but there seemed to be something deeper in the man that set him apart from the average misguided individual.

Robert Zarinsky enjoyed being cruel.

As Zarinsky became a teenager, he learned new ways to inflict pain and misery on others. He gathered together a number of like-minded losers and formed a gang he called the Panthers. The Panthers employed Nazi imagery, even though Zarinsky's father was Jewish, and enjoyed terrorizing the residents around Linden, New Jersey, with acts of arson and vandalism. Zarinsky's reign of terror culminated at the age of twenty-two when he and his friends burned down five lumber yards and desecrated hundreds of tombstones in a Jewish cemetery. Robert claimed insanity and spent some time in a mental hospital.

Zarinsky was not cured; in fact, after Robert was released from the mental hospital he traveled around New Jersey, leaving a trail of bodies in his wake.

A Life of Murder and a Life in Prison

While most of the people in the United States were adjusting to the great social changes of the 1960s, Robert Zarinsky was apparently killing women throughout the state of New Jersey. The change in culture from the somewhat rigid rule structure of the 1950s to the permissive attitudes of the 1960s seemed to be the perfect backdrop for Zarinsky's murderous obsession with girls and young women. Unfortunately, the science needed to catch Zarinsky and other serial killers like him was still a few decades away. DNA profiling would not become commonplace in police investigations until the 1990s, and extensive use of close circuit television cameras was also a couple of decades in the future.

But the Robert Zarinksy case proves that with some patience, modern science has the ability to help identify and capture serial killers.

Although Zarinksy had been convicted of a number of serious felonies before the late 1960s, murder was not yet a crime on his resume of destruction.

In the summer of 1969, seventeen-year-old Rosemary Calandriello was a girl who was trying to find herself in the ever-changing world of the '60s. Calandriello was known to be a good girl, but like most kids her age, she wanted to fit it. Many of Clandriello's friends liked to drink some beer and smoke marijuana, although finding party favors could sometimes be a problem for the broke, underage high school kids.

Enter Robert Zarinksy.

Like a true predator, Zarinsky was known to show up at the parties of people ten years or more younger than him. As a criminal, Zarinsky usually had money, drugs, and a car. He was like the criminal pied piper of New Jersey, which turned out to be fatal for Rosemary Calandriello and a number of other girls and young women.

August 25, 1969, was the last night anyone saw Rosemary Calandrillo, as she seemingly disappeared into thin air, but she was last seen with Robert Zarinsky.

"We had four eyewitnesses who put the girl in his car," said district attorney John Mullaney. "Then we found the car, and the handles on the doors and the windows were missing."

Despite the eyewitnesses' testimonies and the suspicious circumstances of Zarinsky's lost and found car, prosecutors were slow to charge Zarinsky due to a lack of physical evidence and, most importantly, the absence of Calandriello's body.

Despite the lack of a body and very little physical evidence, Mullaney went ahead with the prosecution, and in 1975 Zarinsky earned the dubious distinction of being the first person convicted of murder in the state of New Jersey without a body. Zarinsky appealed the conviction and lost, but by the late 1980s, perhaps believing that he could obtain parole if he "came clean," Zarinsky admitted to murdering Calandriello. In typical sociopathic fashion, he mitigated his responsibility by stating that the murder was accidental. He also vacillated when asked where he disposed of her body: in one interview he said he buried her body in the hills of northwest New Jersey, while in another he claimed to have dumped Calandrillo's corpse in the Atlantic Ocean.

Although the possibility of parole was conceivable for Zarinsky, the time he spent in prison for Rosemary Calandriello's murder gave science and investigators time to catch up with the serial killer's other crimes.

Science Identifies a Serial Killer

The extent of the damage that Robert Zarinksy did to society was not known until fairly recently when scientific advances finally caught up the killer, but the first inkling that he may be a serial killer was revealed because of all things, a family dispute.

While Zarinksy was leading his Panthers gang destroying cemeteries and burning down lumber yards, he also took part in his first homicide. In 1958, when Zarinksy was eighteen, he and his cousin Theodore Schiffer were burglarizing a Pontiac car dealer in Rahway, New Jersey, when they were caught by a police officer.

The cop was a veteran named Charles Bernoskie who happened to see two young men lurking around the parking lot of the Pontiac dealer while he was on patrol. It was a totally random meeting.

Unfortunately for Bernoskie, the random encounter left him dead on the side of the road.

According to witness testimony taken years after the crime, Bernoskie surprised the two miscreants who then attempted to run. In an era long before "police brutality" was a common phrase, Bernoskie then apparently shot at and hit both fleeing suspects, who then returned fire, killing the officer.

"He pissed me off," said Zarinsky according to his sister, Judith Sapsa. "That's why I shot him."

Already seasoned criminals and therefore well aware of what could happen to them if they went to an emergency room, Zarinsky and Schiffer stumbled, bleeding, to Zarinsky's sister Judith Sapsa, who lived nearby. Luckily for the two men, no vital organs were hit, and after Judith and Veronica Zarinsky stitched the two up, they were ready to continue preying on the citizens of New Jersey.

But the murder of Charles Bernoskie was the first time that science caught up with one of Robert Zarinsky's crimes.

In 1999, a fingerprint taken from the crime scene was matched to Schiffer in the Automated Fingerprint Identification System (AFIS). The AFIS database works in much the same way as the CODIS database and essentially served as a template for it; all persons who are fingerprinted for a crime have their prints entered into the AFIS database, which is then used to solve cold cases among other things. It turns out that Schiffer was able to avoid arrest for all of those years, and Zarinsky, perhaps being the more sophisticated criminal, left no fingerprints at the scene. In a strange twist to the crime and an example of the bizarre dynamics of the dysfunctional Zarinsky family, Judith Sapsa implicated her brother as the shooter.

It seems that loyalty in the Zarinsky family only went as far as far as money would take it.

While Robert was serving his sentence for the murder of Rosemary Calandriello, he was able to amass a small fortune through some good investments. Apparently Judith had access to the mutual fund, and as her brother sat in prison, she embezzled a good chunk of it. Once Zarinsky learned of his sister's deception, he turned her in and she was promptly arrested for embezzling. She then saw her chance to get even when Schiffer was arrested for Bernoskie's murder.

The trial of both men turned out to be a lot of finger pointing with very little physical evidence. Schiffer ended up serving only three years for burglary and in 2001 Zarinsky was acquitted of murder. The jury cited the unreliable testimony of Sapsa and Schiffer as one of their primary reasons along with a lack of physical evidence.

But as DNA testing became more sophisticated and the CODIS database became more complete in the 2000s, the totality of Robert Zarinsky's murder spree was bound to surface with the light of day.

Although Zarinsky entered the prison system long before DNA profiling or the CODIS database existed, he, like all long-serving inmates in American prisons, was obliged to give a DNA sample in the 2000s. In the months just before he died in 2008 and in the years since, Zarinsky has been definitively identified through DNA matching as the killer of two girls and considered the likely suspect of at least four others.

After the murder of Charles Bernoskie, Zarinsky appears to have gone into a "cool down" period. Although it appears that Zarinsky did not plan to murder Bernoskie, the act seems to have kindled a dark, murderous desire that was dormant in him.

In 1965, Zarinsky acted on that dark impulse when he savagely raped and beat to death eighteen-year-old Mary Agnes Klinsky near Holmdel, New Jersey. After he was done with the young woman, he tossed her on the side of the road like trash, probably because he believed there was no way he could ever be linked to her.

In 2016, nearly eight years after his death, DNA conclusively linked Zarinsky to Klinsky's murder.

Zarinsky's next known murder took place when he abducted, raped, and murdered thirteen-year-old Jane Durrua on November 4, 1968. Apparently, Jane decided to take a short cut home through a field when she was swooped upon by Zarinksy. Her naked body was found the next day in the field.

Semen stains were taken from Durrua's clothing, but a mix-up in DNA samples originally led to the arrest of another man. After the problem was discovered and rectified, the sample was then matched to Zarinsky, which led to an indictment on March 11, 2008.

Zarinsky died while awaiting trial.

Even though Zarinsky is now dead, his DNA profile may still link him to a host of other murders. Seventeen-year-old Linda Balabanow was found raped and murdered in 1969, after she disappeared on her way to work in Union County, New Jersey. Then there was the case of fourteen-year-old Doreen Carlucci and her friend, fifteen-year-old Joanne Delardo, who were discovered together dead, naked in a field in 1974. The two girls had been raped, beaten, and strangled with an electrical cord.

There was also nineteen-year-old Ann Logan, who was also found raped and beaten to death.

The magnitude of Zarinsky's crimes may never be fully known. Although it may be little comfort to the families of Zarinsky's victims, he spent the last years of his life in fear and pain. In 1999, once his initial case became public and it was announced that he was suspected in the murders of other girls and women in New Jersey, he was transferred from general population at the South Woods state prison to the protected custody block.

It seems that the man who could kill girls and women so easily was no match for the hardened convicts in the New Jersey prison system.

Finally, on November 28, 2008, after suffering from the painful effects of pulmonary fibrosis for some time, Robert Zarinsky died uneventfully in prison.

Although the psychopath took many unanswered questions with him to the grave, DNA profiling and the CODIS database helped prove that he was in fact a serial killer. The finding also helped give closure to some his victims' families.

"We knew he was a serial killer, but there was precious little to prove it," said John Mullaney.

Eventually, the science caught up and was able to uncover Zarinsky's evil deeds.

CHAPTER 12:

THE MURDER OF PATRICIA BEARD

In the United States, the most vulnerable of its citizens are not only protected by the government, but also given assistance. Mentally and physically disabled individuals are often housed in "group homes" where mental health professionals can look after them, and at the same time the residents are encouraged to take jobs in the community in order to realize their full potential. These group homes are safe havens for people with disabilities, as they offer places where the disabled can learn real-world skills as well as live in safety from the often cruel outside world.

Unfortunately for thirty-two-year-old Patricia Beard, a Denver group home could not protect her from the cruel clutches of a killer in 1981.

Patricia Beard was mentally disabled, but also what health care professionals would term a "high-functioning" individual who could work and interact in the larger community. The Denver group home where she lived was one that was there to help its residents with their medications, jobs, and other daily functions, but it was also a home that stressed independence and therefore gave the residents a certain amount of freedom.

Since Patricia Beard was a high functioning resident, staff members of the group home thought nothing when they did not see her for a couple of days. It was a group home, not a jail or halfway house, and its residents could come and go as they pleased. After a couple of more days, Patricia's friends and family started to worry when she did not answer her phone, so one of them went to her apartment and made a grisly discovery.

Patricia Beard was found dead in her room on March 27, 1981.

An investigation of the room by Denver homicide investigators revealed that Beard was strangled to death, and the fact that she was half-naked led them to believe that she was also raped. Vaginal swabs were later taken that confirmed that Patricia was raped before she was killed.

The investigation then turned to creating a list of suspects, but the police were soon discouraged as they met several dead-ends.

Staff at the group home reported seeing no strangers come to the home, and all residents and workers at the home were quickly cleared.

After searching the exterior of the group home, officers determined that the killer crawled into Beard's first floor apartment through a window. Homicide detectives then believed that the killer was a stranger, but probably someone with a record for burglary, sexual assault, or both. Police began their investigation by searching through all their records of burglars and sex offenders whose methods of operations matched the Beard murder. They were quickly let down when no credible matches were made.

Unfortunately, no fingerprints of the killer were lifted from the crime scene, but samples of semen were taken from Beard's vagina and mouth. The biological evidence was stored in an evidence locker where it sat for twenty years.

The Denver Cold Case Unit

The term "cold case" has become such a ubiquitous term in the modern lexicon that few today do not know what it means. Both fictional and documentary television shows that focus on police departments using forensics to capture killers in cases that took place years prior and are therefore considered "cold" are popular fare. Many of these shows depict the work as glamorous, but the reality is that is often tedious, time consuming, and just plain difficult. As depicted on some of these shows, over the last fifteen years, as the science of DNA profiling has progressed with the CODIS system, many police departments have created cold case units to solve murders like Patricia Beard's.

The Denver Cold Case Unit has proved to be one of the best in the world.

The Denver Police Department's cold case unit investigates both unsolved rapes and murders. The result is that the unit has solved more cold cases than any other similar unit in the world!

With such an elite unit working on Patricia Beard's murder, it was only a matter of time until her killer was captured. But first the unit had to get the case, which almost did not happen.

After Patricia Beard's apartment was processed, all of the items relevant to the case, such as the rape kit, were cataloged and then stored in the evidence locker at the Denver Police

Department. There the evidence sat for thirteen years until most of it, with the exception of vaginal swabs, was destroyed to make room for evidence from other cases.

1994 would prove to be an important year in the Patricia Beard case, not just because potential DNA evidence was saved, but also because that was the year that the CODIS database went online.

In 2005, the Denver police department's crime lab and the Denver District Attorney's Office were selected to take part in a national study that investigated the impact of DNA profiling and the CODIS database on cold cases.

With that, the Denver Cold Case Unit was born.

As the unit moved through the remainder of the 2000s and into the 2010s solving cold cases, a detective re-discovered the rape kit from the Patricia Beard murder. Officers entered the evidence into the CODIS system, and in 2013 a match came back for a man named Hector Bencoma-Hinojos.

Bencoma-Hinojos was doing time in a federal prison in Pennsylvania, which therefore required him to give a sample of his DNA profile to the CODIS database. Although the DNA match meant that Bencoma-Hinojos had been sexually intimate with Beard, it did not necessarily mean that he killed or even raped her.

The Denver Cold Case Unit would have to conduct a more thorough investigation of their suspect.

A background check of Bencoma-Hinojos revealed that he was a known criminal and thief who had up until that point avoided doing any major prison time. He was also known to be extremely violent. His wife said that he would routinely threaten and beat her for the slightest indiscretions, and he often carried a knife.

Denver police then traveled to Pennsylvania to interview their captive suspect and, as it turns out, Bencoma-Hinojos' own words proved to be the last nails in his legal coffin.

Bencoma-Hinojos admitted to the authorities that he lived in Denver for several years beginning around 1977 and that he was probably living in the city in 1981, although he was evasive with his answers. The Cold Case Unit detectives then asked Bencoma-Hinojos if he knew Beard, which he answered in the negative. The police then gave their subject one last chance at a way out by showing him a picture of Beard, who was black, and asking him if it were possible that he had sex with the woman. Bencoma-Hinojos vehemently denied ever having sex with Beard and added that he had never had sex with a black woman.

The police caught Bencoma-Hinojos in a lie that the man's own DNA sample could verify!

In 2015, at the age of fifty-five, Hector Bencoma-Hinojos was sentenced to forty eight years in Colorado's Department of Corrections, which will more than likely amount to a life sentence for the middle aged murderer.

Bencoma-Hinojos' conviction proved to be a milestone as it was the 100th case solved by the Denver Police Department's Cold Case Unit.

CONCLUSION

All twelve of the cases examined in this book are amazing and mysterious in their own unique ways. Advances in DNA profiling have helped solve the mysteries of some of these cold case murders, while new eyewitness testimony has contributed to another being solved. In the future, DNA evidence may even identify more victims of the notorious serial killer Robert Zarinsky.

With that said, some mysteries remain.

The disappearance of the Palmer brothers in the vast wilderness of Alaska is a case that neither DNA nor eye-witness testimony appears likely to solve. Unfortunately for the Palmer family, it is as if the Alaskan mountains just swallowed Michael and Chucky whole along with any explanation of what happened.

Eye-witness testimony may help solve the enigmatic coincidence of the Mary Morris murders, but until that time people are left to wonder if the cases were connected or just another bizarre coincidence.

Finally, some cases, such as the Brighton Trunk Murders, defy any logical explanation and serve as proof that anything is possible and as far as man has advanced scientifically speaking, some things are just out of the realm of science.

Yes, the world is an amazing and mysterious place and as this book proves, sometimes crime plays a role in the mysteries of the world.

TRUE CRIME STORIES

12 Shocking True Crime
Murder Cases

True Crime Anthology Vol.2

By
Jack Rosewood
&
Rebecca Lo

INTRODUCTION

Murder happens anywhere, at any time, and the rates of murder are increasing as is the size of the population around the world. Even an economic crisis can trigger an outbreak of sorts of murders. But there are always certain cases that stay in the recesses of your mind, even after years have passed. Why you remember them may depend on the individual case and whether or not you feel some kind of affinity with the victim. Others may stay in your memory because they are so horrific that you just can't forget about them. One thing's for sure— while the victim is being remembered, they are being honored in some small way. Remembering those who have been lost, helps to keep them alive, even if it is just in our memories.

There are twelve cases contained in this book. They range from multiple murders to mistaken identity crimes, as being accused and charged of a murder you didn't commit can also affect you for the rest of your life. There is a chapter on Josef Fritzl, the father who kept his daughter captive for twenty-four years, and the suicide that was found to be a homicide, thanks in part to a popular television program. An alleged angel of death, family murders, police misconduct, and the taking of a child— they are all stories that need to be remembered.

Some of these cases go back a long way, with one being the oldest cold case ever solved. Can you guess what it might be? Fifty years is a long time to wait to see justice done. Or was it?

Twists, turns, puzzles, and psychopathy are all the makings of most of these murder cases. From the youngest victim to the youngest perpetrator, each chapter will draw you further into the history of these horrific crimes.

CHAPTER 1:

MURDER IN THE FRENCH ALPS – IQBAL AL-HILLI AND HER FAMILY

The murders of three family members and what appeared to be a random cyclist, as well as the wounding of two children, created shockwaves around the world. The nationalities of the victims, the remoteness of the attack, and the fact that two little girls were left to hide amongst the dead, brought law agencies around the world into the investigation. There were so many questions that needed to be answered—why them? How did they know they would be there? Was the cyclist involved? Was it an international hit? And was there a lot more to the story than anyone had realized?

From Scenic Views to Crime Scene

The French Alps is perhaps one of the most beautiful locations in the world and is a popular destination for vacationers. It is no wonder that Iqbal Al-Hilli, her husband Saad, their two daughters, and her elderly mother Suhaila Al-Allaf too decided to choose the Alps for their family vacation. What would ensue, however, would dramatically alter the pristine landscape that was to become one of absolute horror on September 5, 2012.

On a remote scenic vista near historic Lake Annecy sat the BMW the family was using for their trip. Inside the car were the bodies of Iqbal, Saad, and Suhaila, all of whom had been shot. One of their daughters was found outside the car. The seven year old who had been shot in the shoulder and also had a wound to the head. At the time of the discovery, nobody was aware that there was another young daughter. She was hiding beneath her mother's legs in the back of the car and remained hidden for some eight hours, even while the local police were on the scene, until she was finally discovered unhurt.

Further along the road a short distance lay the body of a cyclist, Frenchman Sylvain Mollier. He had reportedly been shot seven times, though nobody had a clue why or how he was tied in with the murdered family. Each of the victims inside the car had been shot twice in the head, and evidence at the scene showed that twenty-five shots in total were fired. The engine of the car was still running when discovered, and the car had been shifted into reverse, with the back wheels spinning in the loose sandy gravel.

A Puzzle with Too Many Angles

Initially, the case was handled by the local police, called the Gendarme, and then the National Gendarme joined in. There were so many angles to the tragedy that it was never going to be an easy one to solve. From the nationalities of the victims to their families, their lines of work, and links to a Middle East dictator, there were so many possible motives that eventually France and Britain created a joint investigation team to investigate.

Saad Al-Hilli

One of the first leads investigated was the background of Saad Al-Hilli. Originally from Iraq, Saad had once worked as an engineer on what were considered to be sensitive topics in Iraq, and he subsequently was employed in the nuclear and satellite technology industry in England. Satellites, nuclear technology, and ties with Iraq alone were enough to consider the murders an act of assassination with Saad being the main target.

There were also suspicious circumstances surrounding the family of Saad, namely his father and his brother Zaid. There had been a claim that £840,000 had been placed in a Swiss bank account in Saad's father's name by the regime of Saddam Hussein. There were even reports leaked that showed Saad may have had access to Saddam Hussein's bank accounts. Could the murders have been a contract hit related to the dictator?

To further add fuel to the theory of a family-related hit, his brother Zaid came under investigation due to a feud regarding a family inheritance. Zaid was eventually arrested in June 2013, but was subsequently released due to a lack of evidence, despite the suggestion that he tried to commit fraud by altering his father's will. However, suspicion always remained that he may have had a part to play in the murders.

Sylvain Mollier

Was Sylvain the innocent cyclist who was in the wrong place at the wrong time? Or was he the intended target and the family were the ones caught in the crossfire? Similar to Saad, Sylvain had also worked in the nuclear industry, and this was considered a possible lead. However, it was later substantiated that he was simply a welder and had no access to any delicate nuclear information, so this was later deemed unlikely to be the reason behind the murders. It seemed he really was just in the wrong place at the wrong time.

The Work of a Serial Killer?

This was perhaps one of the more far-fetched theories, with very little data to back it up. The detectives surmised that the murders were committed by a psychopath acting alone who perhaps had a dislike of tourists. This theory came about because of the similarities with a previous murder of a tourist in July 2012. There was never any real movement on this lead, and it was considered by most to be inconclusive.

Mystery Motorcyclist

A man riding a motorcycle was seen in the vicinity of the crime, but his identity was unknown. It wasn't until 2015 that the man in question was located by the police, and he was completely ruled out. He had simply been an innocent man out riding a motorcycle.

The Legionnaire

Patrice Menegaldo was an ex-soldier of the French Foreign Legion who found himself on the suspect list. He subsequently committed suicide, though the reason behind this is not clear. It is also not clear as to why he was ever considered a suspect, and despite the State Prosecutor at the time stating he was, the police denied he was ever considered a primary suspect.

Iqbal Al-Hilli

Initially the investigation focused on the background of her husband Saad and his potential links to both the nuclear industry and Saddam Hussein. Her background had seemed fairly straightforward, or so the investigators thought. However, it would later come out that she had a secret that very few people knew about, and this would lead to a further coincidental death and conspiracy.

A Secret Husband?

Before her marriage to Saad, Iqbal had once been married to an American gentleman named Jim Thompson. What had appeared to be simply a marriage of convenience to enable Iqbal to get her U.S. Green Card was perhaps more than anyone realized.

During her time in the U.S., Iqbal went by the name of Kelly, and upon meeting ex-cop Jim in 1999, he agreed to help her out by marrying her so that she could live and work there. The marriage was said to be platonic yet very caring. However, Iqbal discovered that her dentistry qualifications weren't accepted by the U.S. and ended the marriage just months later. Jim reluctantly drove her to the airport and said goodbye.

Her next contact with Jim was in 2003, when she declared she had fallen in love with another man, Saad, and she needed a divorce. Jim happily granted her the divorce, and she went on to marry the man she would later die with. But the story between Iqbal and Jim didn't end there.

Jim's sister Judy Weatherly would later state that Jim and Iqbal had stayed in touch throughout the nine years she was married to Saad. Regular emails went back and forth, and Iqbal's family knew nothing about it at all. They didn't even know she had once been married to Jim. There has even been suggestion that the divorce was never legalized, which would mean Iqbal had entered her marriage to Saad as a bigamist. So what was the importance of this secret relationship in relation to the murders? Here's where it gets even more bizarre and interesting.

Death by Coincidence

On exactly the same day that Iqbal and her family were slaughtered in the French Alps, her former husband Jim died at the wheel of his car, presumably from a heart attack. This extraordinary coincidence would lead the French investigators to question whether or not the deaths were related in some way. Jim may have been sixty years and had a history of high blood pressure, but the timing of his death seemed too much of a freak occurrence, considering what had happened to his ex-wife at that same point in time.

To further add to the speculation, he had allegedly called his sister Judith two weeks before his death and instructed her that if anything happened to him she was to go through his room, as there was something there that would be surprising. Judith followed through with his wishes, but the only thing she found was a box full of photos and information about his marriage to Iqbal. It seemed he clearly wanted people to know they had been married, but for what reason? Was he trying to say he had been forewarned or knew he was at risk of being killed?

The death of Jim became increasingly important to the French authorities, who started to question whether he had also been murdered due to something between him and Iqbal. The most likely scenario, according to the authorities, was that he had been poisoned, which would mimic a heart attack. They set about requesting an exhumation to test for the presence of poisons, but Judith would not allow it. The FBI also supported the request for an exhumation, but the American authorities refused, believing there were not sufficient grounds to commit such an act. As recent as 2015, the FBI has considered making a further request for the exhumation to take place, and questions are still not answered.

Murder Unsolved

To date, there has been no further progress in identifying the motive or the perpetrator of the tragic murders of the Al-Hilli family and the cyclist, Sylvain Mollier. Though there have been a number of theories and leads, they veer off in so many directions that it has proven impossible so far to narrow them down to one plausible suspect. Did Saddam Hussein's regime put a contract on Saad's head because he had accessed bank accounts he shouldn't have? Or did he have too much information regarding satellites and nuclear technologies in the Middle East?

Did Saad's brother Zaid have his own relatives executed over an inheritance? Or had he been stealing money from the family account and felt the need to remove any potential possibility of being discovered? After all, family feuds can often lead to violence. But to kill your own brother, his wife, her mother, and leave the two little girls orphans is a pretty big stretch. Not to mention the poor cyclist who just happened to come along at the wrong time.

Another thing to consider is that the girls were not killed. If it was a contract hit, why would they have left living witnesses? Sure, the girls were only young, but who knows what they may have seen, heard or experienced? The killer or killers had time to shoot each victim in the head twice, yet only one of the girls had injuries—a bullet to the shoulder and a head injury from being pistol-whipped. It's true that the youngest of the girls was hiding underneath the legs of her dead mother, but an assassin that knows who the family is and where they are going to be at that present moment in time would surely know there were two children also traveling in the car. Why were they spared? A heartless, psychopathic killer isn't going to worry about sparing the children—they simply wouldn't care.

Finally, strong consideration should be given to the possibility of Jim, Iqbal's first husband, having been murdered on the very same day. Sure, coincidences do occur, but this one is just so bizarre that it is too good to be true. What did he know? Had Iqbal been confiding even more secrets to Jim? Why did he mention the possibility of something happening to him just weeks before he died? Unfortunately, there have been many questions and few answers in this case, and at this point in time they are no closer to solving it. The authorities involved in this case still hope for that major breakthrough that will put an end to this terrible mystery.

CHAPTER 2:

THE VILLISCA AXE MURDERS

In 1912, Villisca was a small Midwestern town in Iowa with a population of just 2,500. Despite its size, it was a busy little town with trains coming and going every day, businesses up and down the streets, and it was home to the first publicly funded armory in the whole state. For many, the name 'Villisca' meant 'pleasant view' or 'pretty place'. But regardless of the business successes and the beauty of the town, its history would be forever marred by one single event—the brutal and horrifying murder of eight people in one house, on one night, with an axe.

The Moore's

The Moore family was well liked in the community, and their affluence was well known. The members of the family were Josiah, who was 43 at the time, his wife Sarah, aged 39, and their children, Herman Montgomery, aged 11, Mary Katherine, 10, Arthur Boyd, 7, and Paul Vernon, 5. They were regular church attendees, and on the evening of June 9, 1912, the children had been participating in the Presbyterian Church's Children's Day Program. This program lasted until 9:30 p.m., and the Moore family invited two young girls, Ina Mae Stillinger, aged 8, and her sister Lena Gertrude, who was 12 years old, to stay the night in their home. All walked back to the home of the Moores, arriving somewhere between 9:45 to 10 p.m. No one is sure what time the family and their guests retired to bed that evening, or what if anything was amiss in the house when they got home. What is known, however, is that what did occur during the night in that house would become legendary, for all the wrong reasons.

A Gruesome Scene

On the morning of June 10, the next door neighbor, Mary Peckham, found it strange that the family next door was not up and about at 7 a.m. as they usually were. She was used to hearing and seeing the family members as they started their morning chores, but they hadn't appeared, and the curtains were all closed. Mary decided to check on the family and went and knocked on the door, but nobody responded. She tried to open the door, but it was still locked. Fearing something was very wrong, she called Josiah's brother Ross to investigate. Oddly, she first let the Moore's chickens out of their coop—goodness knows why.

Ross arrived at the house, and like Mary he knocked on the door, shouting out in the hopes that someone inside would hear him. On receiving no response, he proceeded to unlock the door with his copy of the key to the house. Mary waited anxiously on the porch as Ross entered the house and made his way into the guest bedroom. The scene that greeted him was horrific—the bodies of the Stillinger sisters dead in the bed. Moore instructed Mary to call the local officer, Hank Horton, who arrived within a short period of time. It was Horton who further investigated the rest of the house, finding body after body of the Moore family, all with horrific head wounds. In the guest room where the bodies of the Stillinger sisters lay was a bloodied axe, and that was immediately identified as the murder weapon.

Though the injuries to each of the victims were gruesome, it was Josiah who seemed to have been dealt the most vicious blows. Unlike the others who had been bludgeoned to death with the blunt end of the axe, it was the sharp end that had been used on Josiah. In fact, his wounds were so horrific that his eyes were missing in his cut-up face. Gouge marks in the ceilings of the bedrooms had been created by the swinging of the axe; in some cases, these gouges were in the center of the room, not near the beds, and it was surmised that the killer must have been in some sort of wild frenzy, swinging the axe triumphantly after each kill.

The pillows on the beds were soaked in blood and spattered with brain matter. By the time the first doctor entered the house, the blood had congealed into a jelly, and clots were noticeable, and this indicated they had been killed somewhere shortly after midnight. Each of the victims had their faces covered with their bedclothes, and all lay in their beds as though they had been killed while sleeping, except for Lena Stillinger. Her body showed defensive wounds, suggesting she had tried to fight off the attacker. Her nightgown had been pushed up and her underwear removed, and her body had been posed in a sexual manner. Naturally consideration was given to the possibility she had been sexually assaulted or raped, but this was never determined without a doubt.

There were other strange things about the crime scene that made no sense at all. Although it is normal to pull the curtains closed on the windows, those which did not have curtains were covered with clothing that had belonged to the victims. Every mirror in the house had also been covered, which was truly bizarre. At the foot of Josiah and Sarah's bed sat a kerosene lamp with the chimney missing and the wick turned to black. The chimney was eventually found beneath a dresser. Another lamp was found at the end of the guest bed, where the bodies of the Stillinger girls lay. It too had the chimney missing. The axe itself, although covered in blood, showed signs that the killer had tried to wipe away the blood to no avail. The axe was found to belong to Josiah. In the bedroom downstairs, a small piece of keychain was found that didn't seem to belong to anyone in the house. On the table in the kitchen was a pan containing bloody water and a plate of food that hadn't been touched. Up in the attic, two cigarette butts were located, and it was assumed that the killer (perhaps killers) had waited up there for the family to return home. This was perhaps the most terrifying piece of evidence—to think that this innocent family returned home following a pleasant evening only to be ambushed by someone waiting inside.

Who Were the Suspects?

There were numerous suspects on the list, and one was even arrested and tried for the crime, though eventually he was acquitted. They ranged from transients to a reverend, and even a serial killer, but nobody was ever held accountable and brought to justice for this horrific massacre of the Moore family and the Stillinger girls.

Andrew Sawyer

Naturally, any transients or strangers were considered suspicious during the investigation into the murders. This is generally because people as a rule don't trust strangers, and nobody wants to consider that maybe it was someone they knew. In small towns in particular, people are more wary of those they don't know. One such man that fit this bill was Andrew Sawyer.

There was never any concrete evidence to suggest Sawyer had played a part in the killings. Instead, he was brought to light by a gentleman who worked for the railroad and had interacted with Sawyer on the morning of the murders in nearby Creston. Thomas Dyer alleged that Sawyer had appeared around 6 a.m. that morning looking for work. He was dressed in a brown suit, was shaven, his pants were wet almost up to his knees, and his shoes were covered in mud. Workers were highly sought after, so he was hired there and then. Later that evening, Sawyer apparently bought a newspaper with the murders broadcast across the front page, and he went off alone to read it.

Apparently, Sawyer was very interested in the murders, and he talked about them often with his fellow workers. Even more strange, he had a habit of sleeping with his axe next to him. He would later tell Dyer that he had been in Villisca the night of the murders but had left for fear of being considered a suspect. When considering all of the strange behaviors he had exhibited, Dyer handed Sawyer over to the sheriff on June 18, 1912.

Despite the statements Sawyer had made to his work colleagues and the intense interest he seemed to show in the murders, even placing himself in town on the night in question, it would later be proven that he was innocent. On investigation, it turned out that Sawyer had been arrested on that very night in a town called Osceola, also in Iowa, for vagrancy. Therefore, he had an alibi.

The Reverend George Kelly

Kelly was a man with a disturbing background who happened to be at the very same Children's Day services the Moore family and the Stillinger sisters attended that day, June 9, 1912. Born in England, Kelly was a traveling minister who many regarded as being rather odd. It was claimed that he had suffered some type of mental breakdown when he was younger, and his adult behavior included lewd acts such as peeping and trying to get young girls to pose for him in the nude. Strangely, he left Villisca somewhere between 5 a.m. and 5:30 a.m., just hours after the murders had occurred and before the bodies were found.

Over the following weeks, he showed a strong fascination with the case. He began to write letters to the investigators, the police, and even the mourning family members. As expected, this behavior seemed suspicious to the investigators, and they in turn wrote back asking if Kelly happened to know anything about the killings. Kelly replied that he may have witnessed the crimes being committed and had heard sounds that evening. However, due to his history of mental illness, the police were unsure whether he was recalling facts because he was involved or whether he was just making it all up.

Kelly was arrested on a different matter in 1914, after having sent obscene material to a woman who had applied to work for him. As a result he was sent to a mental health hospital in Washington, which left the police unsure if he was the killer or not. However, in 1917 they decided to interrogate Kelly again, and following several hours of questioning, Kelly confessed to the crimes. Later he would recant this confession, claiming to be innocent after all. Two trials followed, and the jury obviously agreed with him, as the first trial resulted in a hung jury and the second led to an acquittal.

State Senator Frank F. Jones

As a suspect, Senator Jones was perhaps the least likely to have been behind the murders. However, there was a rumor that he had hired William 'Blackie' Mansfield to commit the crimes following an issue that had arisen between the Senator and Josiah Moore. Josiah at one time had worked for the Senator at his implement shop for several years and then left his employment so he could open up his own store. This resulted in the Senator losing a lot of his customers to Josiah, including a very lucrative dealership with John Deere. There were also rumors around town that Josiah and the Senator's daughter-in-law had an affair, though this was never substantiated. Would a man such as the State Senator have ordered the assassination of an entire family over something such as lost business and possible adultery? The investigators clearly didn't think so, as this matter was not taken any further, at least where the Senator was concerned. Mansfield, on the other hand, was an entirely different matter.

William 'Blackie' Mansfield

Mansfield came to light as a potential suspect not only because of the rumor of his being hired by the Senator, but also because of murders he subsequently committed following the massacre in the Moore household. Two years after the murders in Villisca, Mansfield was suspected of murdering his wife, child, father-in-law and mother-in-law in very similar circumstances, which made the authorities take a much closer look at Mansfield. He was linked by circumstance to the axe murders in Colorado

Springs just nine months before Villisca and another axe murder in Ellsworth, Kansas. He was also suspected of being the perpetrator of axe murders in Paola, Kansas, just four days before the tragedy at Villisca. Furthermore, he was a prime suspect in the axe murders in Illinois of Jennie Miller and Jennie Peterson. More axe murders occurring around the same time period were also considered to be the work of one man. The similarities between all of these murders were spine-tingling.

Each of these murders was committed in the same manner, which would indicate they were done by the same person. All victims were attacked with an axe, and the mirrors in each home had been covered. A kerosene lamp was left burning with the chimney removed at the foot of each bed. A basin containing bloody water was found at each scene, where the murdered had obviously tried to clean himself. Gloves were worn at each crime scene, leaving no trace of fingerprints. The coincidences were just too good to be true, and although we have more access to media information these days, back then the chances of there being a copycat killer or killers roaming the streets were less likely.

In 1916, the Grand Jury agreed to embark on an investigation and Mansfield was arrested. He was transported from Kansas City to Montgomery County to face questioning. Despite all of the evidence that seemed to indicate he was the murderer, Mansfield was found to have a legitimate alibi for the night of the murders in Villisca and so was set free without being charged. He would then bring a lawsuit against the detective who had pursued him as a suspect, Detective James Wilkerson. Mansfield won his case and was awarded the staggering amount of $2,225. This was a huge amount in those days. Some speculated that the Senator played a part in getting Mansfield released, but this was never proven.

Henry Lee Moore

Henry, who was no relation to Josiah Moore and his family, had been convicted of a double axe murder months after the murders in Villisca. Henry had killed his mother and his grandmother, and there was much suspicion that Henry was actually a serial killer. The crimes were very similar, especially as the same type of weapon was used, but there was never any evidence to link him to the Moore family murders. He was always considered a suspect, however, and he was never completely ruled out.

Fourteen Witnesses Called to Coroner's Inquest

Remarkably, the coroner called the jury together and began the inquest on June 11, 1912, just two days after the murders had taken place. Nowadays it can take months or years for an inquest to take place, let alone in the same week! Anyway, the county coroner at the time was Dr. Linquist, and he and the members of the jury all visited the Moore house to view the scene and the bodies before they were removed. A temporary morgue was set up at the local fire station, and the bodies were finally moved there around 2 a.m. on the June 10.

A total of fourteen witnesses were called to testify at the inquest, and they were as follows:

- Mary Peckham—the neighbor who raised the alarm that something was wrong at the house
- Ed Selley—an employee of Josiah, Ed had arrived to take care of the animals

- Dr. J. Clark Cooper—the first doctor to enter the house following the discovery
- Jessie Moore—Ross Moore's wife, who took the call from Mary
- Dr. F.S. Williams—the doctor who examined the bodies
- Edward Landers—was staying just up the road at his mother's house and claimed he heard a noise around 11 p.m.
- Ross Moore—Josiah's brother, the first person to gain entry to the house
- Fenwick Moore—also Josiah's brother
- Marshall Hank Horton—the first officer to enter the house
- John Lee Van Gilder—Josiah's nephew
- Harry Moore—Josiah's brother
- Joseph Stillinger— the father of the murdered Stillinger girls
- Blanche Stillinger—sister of the murdered Stillinger girls
- Charles Moore—another of Josiah's brothers

Most of the witnesses were called to testify regarding what they had seen when entering the house that day. The descriptions given by some were gruesome to say the least, but their testimony was all consistent. Josiah's brothers were called largely to speak of any troubles Josiah may have had or been in, such as business problems. None could say that they were aware of any issues or of anyone who wished to cause the family such terrible harm. One brother, Charles, was asked to testify regarding whether the axe belonged to Josiah or not. Although he couldn't say it was for sure, he did state that Josiah owned one similar. It must have been a terrible burden on both the Moore and Stillinger families to have to endure the inquest so quickly after the tragedy. They barely had time to digest what had happened before being thrust into a courtroom to discuss it, and the details must have been truly shocking. Particularly for the father of the two little Stillinger girls who had simply gone to a friend's house for the night.

Deathbed and Jailhouse Confessions

On March 19, 1917, a reverend by the name of J.J. Burris, who was the pastor of the Church of Christ in Oklahoma, traveled to Red Oak because of a deathbed confession he had received. Burris was subpoenaed by the grand jury of Montgomery County to give evidence regarding this confession of the murders of the Moore family. Burris had claimed that a man whose name he could not remember had summoned him to his hotel room so that he could confess his sins before dying. This took place in July 1913, just over a year after the murders had been committed.

Burris stated that when he arrived at the man's room, he could tell straight away that he was near death, and despite his physical state, the man began to talk the minute he entered the room. The man claimed that he had committed many sins, but the worst was the murders in Villisca. He had been living in the town at the time, working in the blacksmith industry, and his sister had been married to a physician in Villisca before moving to Radersburg. He was unable to speak for long due to his deteriorating condition, and as such was incapable of giving any details. Burris estimated the man to be around twenty-five years old, and it was believed he had part ownership in a blacksmith business in Radersburg.

Because the story was unclear, Detective Wilkerson decided that it would not stand up in court, as too little information was available. The man who had made the confession was dead and unable to stand trial anyway. The story was pushed aside as irrelevant.

George Meyers Confesses in Jail

In March 1931, a prisoner in a county jail in Detroit who was awaiting sentencing for burglary made a startling confession, stating he was the one who had committed the axe murders in Villisca. Meyers had been under interrogation for around five hours by detectives at the time of his confession, following an anonymous tip that he was the man they were looking for. It was believed that Meyers' fingerprints had been found at the murder scene; however, this was unlikely as no fingerprints were found in the Moore house.

Meyers' confession stated that he had been hired to kill the family by a businessman, though he could not recall his name. The price on offer was $5,000—a huge amount. He claimed his name had been given to these people through acquaintances in the Kansas City underworld. This acquaintance escorted him to Villisca to meet with the man who wished to hire him. He was shown the house where the family lived and told to kill them all. A deposit payment of $2,000 was given, and Meyers was told he would receive the rest after the job was done. Meyers then entered the house shortly after midnight and slaughtered the two adults and four children with an axe. When meeting with the businessman afterwards he was told he would have to wait for the rest of the money. Meyers decided it was best to flee town before the sun came up for fear of being caught.

Now, if you read that carefully, you would see what the problem was with Meyers' confession. George Meyers only confessed to killing six people that night—two adults and four children. But there were eight killed in that house, not six. He flatly denied killing the Stillinger girls, only the Moore family. Although there had been a witness story that claimed three men had been overhead talking in the forest near the house the night of the murders about committing the crime, and this seems to fit with Meyers, his acquaintance, and the businessman, there is no way Meyers would have gotten the number of victims wrong. Therefore, it was decided that this confession was nonsense, and no further action was taken against him for the crime. To date, nobody has ever been charged with these murders, so the case remains unsolved.

CHAPTER 3:

THE DISAPPEARANCE OF STACY PETERSON AND CHRISTIE MARIE CALES

One day she was there, the next she had vanished without a trace. The story of Stacy Peterson and her disappearance was one that would baffle investigators. How could someone simply vanish off the face of the earth? However, Stacy had the misfortune of being married to a man who was not at all what he seemed—Drew Peterson, police officer, husband, and murderer. Was he behind her disappearance?

The Troubled Life of Stacy

Stacy had lived a terrible childhood, fraught with fighting parents, alcohol abuse, violence, and neglect. Her mother seemed incapable of doing anything except drinking a case of beer each day and lying on the couch while the children were left to fend for themselves. They had already lost one child in a house fire and then lost a baby to SIDs later on. These tragedies most likely contributed to the volatile household and Stacy's mother's regular stays in both jail and mental hospitals. Despite all of this, Stacy was able to stay on the right path, and she graduated from high school early at just sixteen years of age.

With a dream of becoming a nurse but unable to afford the education, Stacy took on a variety of odd jobs. When she was seventeen in 2001, she was working at a hotel as a desk clerk when she met the man she would later marry, police officer Drew Peterson. Drew was 47 years old and on his third marriage when they met, but that didn't stop either of them. Stacy saw in Drew the father figure she had never really had and a chance at a secure life. Drew divorced his wife in October 2003, and eight days later he married Stacy.

The first child they had together was a boy called Anthony, who was named after Stacy's father. She was right in her element in her role as wife and mother, and she was an excellent housewife. She believed she had a good marriage, probably because she was young and naïve. Drew would call her constantly when she went out, even if she was just going to the grocery store. He would not let her get a job, he did nothing to take care of the baby, and he more or less tried to control every aspect of her life.

In 2004, Drew's ex-wife Kathleen Savio was found dead, apparently having had an accident in the bathtub. Stacy was quick to defend her husband against any allegations that he had been behind the death, and she even provided an alibi for him. By then she had another child, Lacy, who was named after her sister who passed away, so young Stacy had two children to worry about and was desperate to keep the family together. She would do or say anything to protect her husband.

When Stacy was twenty-three, following the loss of her sister Tina to cancer, she started to make changes in her life. She started to take the children to Bible studies, had taken on a job as an Avon sales rep, and was generally taking better care of herself and her appearance. This all went against Drew's instructions, and he certainly wasn't pleased. But by now Stacy had started to question whether her husband had been involved in the death of his wife Kathleen. By October 2007, she had decided she wanted a divorce.

Just one week later, on October 28, Stacy had vanished.

Gone Without a Trace

On the day of October 28, 2007, Stacy was meant to go and help her sister with some painting, but she never arrived. She sent a text message that Sunday morning at 10:15 saying she wasn't ready to get up out of bed yet. There was no further contact. From then onward, nobody would ever hear from Stacy or see her again. She literally just vanished without a trace.

Drew claimed Stacy had called him that same night from an airport, saying she had met another man and was leaving. Despite this story, her family reported her missing, as they knew she wouldn't have gone without her kids. Family and friends also knew that Stacy had been making plans to leave Drew, so there was no chance she would just up and go without carrying those plans through.

While the authorities and numerous volunteers scoured the area for any trace of Stacy, Drew seemed to be treating it with very little concern. He made flippant remarks and treated the whole situation as if it was a bit of a joke. When questioned about Stacy wanting a divorce, he claimed she asked him all the time for one, depending on her menstrual cycle. Drew Peterson was showing a side of himself that people hadn't seen before, and it was very unpleasant.

The night before her disappearance, Stacy had been hanging out with her sister, Cassandra Cales, and had said to her sister that if anything ever happened to her it was Drew that did it. Cassandra desperately pleaded with her sister to leave with her right then and there, but Stacy said she couldn't leave the children.

Morphey's Story

Thomas Morphey was the stepbrother of Drew, and he had quite the story to tell. The only difficulty was getting people to listen. Morphey stated he was involved in conversations with Drew over a period of two days, starting on October 27, wherein he was convinced Drew was planning to murder someone. It all started with Drew arriving at Morphey's residence and asking him to go for a ride to a nearby park. Allegedly, Drew asked him if he loved him enough to kill for him, to which Morphey replied no, he would be unable to live with himself. Drew then asked if he could live with himself knowing about it. To this question Morphey replied yes, further adding that they had already assumed Drew had killed Kathleen.

Drew then proceeded to tell Morphey that Stacy had been unfaithful and that he had seen her out with other men, and something had to be done about it. He then drove them to a storage facility and asked Morphey to rent a locker for him, and told him if he put it in his own name, he would be paid $2,000. Assuming Drew was planning to store a body there, Morphey was concerned that it would smell. Drew replied that it would be in a sealed container, so it wouldn't be a problem. It was at that very point Morphey knew Drew was going to murder someone, but he didn't realize it would be Stacy. He thought it would be the man she was allegedly having an affair with.

Despite Drew's persuasion, Morphey couldn't rent the locker, as he didn't have any identification with him. He returned home, and after a few hours he called Drew and told him he didn't want to be involved in anything, and Drew stated he respected his wishes. However, the following day Drew arrived at Morphey's residence completely unannounced and again asked to go for a ride to the park. When they reached the park, Morphey was given a cell phone and told not to answer it. Drew then left, leaving Morphey to wonder what was going on.

The phone rang twice, forty-five minutes after Drew had left Morphey in the park. The caller ID showed the calls were coming from Stacy's cell phone, and he suddenly realized that Drew was setting it up to murder Stacy. He assumed Drew was driving around to various locations so the cell phone would ping off different towers when police investigated. An hour later, Drew came back, picked up Morphey, and took back the cell phone. Morphey again told Drew that he didn't want to be involved and that he wanted to go home. Drew said he just needed to pop over to the house for a minute. Despite his disagreement, Morphey went along with him.

Morphey waited outside the house, and out came Drew with a large blue barrel. Drew was unable to get it down the stairs on his own, so Morphey had to help him. They then loaded it into the back of the truck. Morphey was driven home and instructed that 'none of this ever happened'. Despite not actually assisting with the murder of Stacy, the fact that he had been involved with the suspicious phone calls and had helped to carry the barrel which most likely contained her body, created so much guilt that the following day Morphey attempted suicide. His wife rushed him to the hospital, and once he had recovered, he was taken to the police by his brother. Even though he had been somewhat involved, he was granted immunity from prosecution and placed under police protection for six months while he waited to be called by the grand jury.

The lawyer acting for Drew, Joel Brodsky described Morphey's story as a tale dreamt up by an alcohol and drug addict. He did not believe Morphey was a credible witness because of his problems with addiction and therefore would be unlikely to ever be called to testify.

Kathleen Savio

While married to Vicki Connolly, Drew embarked on an affair with Kathleen Savio. His marriage to Vicki was falling apart due to his infidelities and controlling behavior, and they divorced in 1992. Soon after the divorce was finalized, Kathleen and Drew were married. They would go on to have two sons, Kristopher and Thomas. The marriage was not a happy one for very long, and in 2002 Kathleen got a protection order against her husband due to physical abuse. By 2003, Drew was involved with Stacy, and he and Kathleen divorced. However, the financial issues of the marriage were never finalized, and they were still trying to come to an agreement in April 2004. A hearing was set, but Kathleen would never attend, as by March 1, 2004, she was dead.

Kathleen's body was found in her bathtub at home. There was no water in the bathtub, and there were some injuries to her body, yet the physician who performed the initial autopsy claimed it was an accidental death. He surmised that she had slipped in the bathtub and hit her head, drowning, and that was the cause of death. Drew had seemed to get away with it, until his fourth wife Stacy disappeared and the police decided to take another look at the death. Stacy had admitted to at least three people in the days leading up to her disappearance that she believed Drew had murdered Kathleen, so this accusation was taken very seriously.

A second autopsy was conducted on Kathleen, with surprising results. The front of her body was covered in bruises, and Dr. Larry Blum believed these were fresh. There were scrape marks down her back, and he brushed away the initial autopsy report stating these were from rubbing against the back of the bathtub as ridiculous. The surface of the tub was incredibly smooth, and there was nothing there that could have made those marks. The back of Kathleen's head had a wound that had split the skin but not the skull beneath. Blum determined this was most likely from a direct blow. His final determination was that Kathleen had been subjected to a brutal attack shortly before her death and that her death was not an accident at all.

Another Wife Murdered? The Trial of Drew Peterson

Drew was indicted on two counts of first degree murder in 2009, in relation to Kathleen Savio's death. He was held in custody from May and stayed there until his trial. A lot of the evidence against Drew would normally be considered hearsay, but due to a special law passed in Illinois in 2008, exceptions could be made in some cases.

The trial began in July 2012, after much negotiation regarding the secondhand witness statements and as to what would be allowed and what would not. Of the fourteen statements handed to the judge, only eight were approved for use during the trial. The prosecution team had requested a mistrial, but Peterson himself withdrew this request, as he wanted the current jury to hear his case. The trial would last months, until the final verdict was given on September 6, 2012. Drew Peterson was found guilty and convicted of the first degree murder of Kathleen and was sentenced to sixty years in prison. But that wasn't to be the end of courtrooms for Drew.

Drew was charged of trying to organize a hit on the Will County State's Attorney James Glasgow in February 2015. This had come about following a year of Drew's activities between September 2013 and December 2014, when he had been trying to arrange for the attorney's murder. He was charged with one count of solicitation of murder and one count of solicitation of murder for hire.

Now that Drew had been found guilty of the murder of his ex-wife Kathleen, the family and friends of Stacy Peterson began to push for further investigation into her disappearance. It seemed more than likely that if he could murder one wife to be rid of a perceived problem, then surely it would be easy for him to do the same to another wife. To this day, he still claims she ran away with another man.

Disappearance of Her Mother—Christie Marie Cales

Christie's life had been one of pain, suffering and addiction. Having tragically lost two children, Christie embarked on a downward spiral that would see her consumed by an addiction and having to go into mental institutions for treatment. She seemed completely incapable of dealing with daily life, and her children to husband Anthony Cales were left to take care of themselves. The marriage continued to deteriorate, and Christie had a habit of disappearing sometimes for weeks. In 1990, Christie was arrested for stealing cigarettes from a store and was then caught driving while under the influence in alcohol. The family was in serious trouble, and financial matters had reached the point where there were two foreclosures on the family home.

That same year, Anthony filed for divorce, unable to cope with Christie's behavior and the effects on the family any longer. Initially Christie contested the divorce, but she repeatedly missed the court hearings, and Anthony was granted full and sole custody of the children. Christie moved in with other family members, and eventually Anthony and the children moved to Florida. Despite the distance, Christie was still able to see the children from time to time.

Christie met another man and moved in with him. In 1998, Christie left the house carrying her bible and purse and was never seen or heard from again. There were different witness statements, with some saying Christie had said she was going to church, which would make sense given the bible she was carrying, and others saying she was going shopping. Because Christie had a history of disappearing now and then, it wasn't taken too seriously at first. However, her daughters Stacy, Cassandra, and Tina, all believed she was murdered, and they suspected Christie's boyfriend of being the killer. They tried to make a case with the local police, but they failed to agree, and no investigation was undertaken.

It is so ironic and tragic that both mother and daughter would disappear, leaving friends and family to wonder what ever happened to them. One thing is for sure—both are most likely to have been murdered.

CHAPTER 4:

LUCIA DE BERK – ANGEL OF DEATH?

Unlike the previous chapters where the focus was on a murder victim, in this case the victim is still very much alive. Lucia de Berk was a pediatric nurse in her home country of the Netherlands, and due to an investigation into unexplained deaths of patients in her care, she was subsequently arrested, charged, and found guilty of murder and attempted murder. However, Lucia was not the angel of death so many suspected at all. Instead, she was a victim of a terrible miscarriage of justice which almost saw her put behind bars for the rest of her natural life.

Accused of Seven Cases of Murder and Three Cases of Attempted Murder

Lucia was working as a pediatric nurse at the Juliana Children's Hospital in The Hague, Netherlands, when an investigation into suspicious deaths during hospital admissions was undertaken. On September 4, 2001, a baby died suddenly while in the hospital, and this triggered an investigation into any unexpected deaths or resuscitation attempts. It was found that there had been nine incidents between September 2000 and September 2001, which originally were thought to be natural deaths but on further inspection of the records appeared to be highly suspicious.

One nurse had been on duty on the occasion of each of these deaths—Lucia. At the time, she was responsible for giving medication and managing the care of each patient. To the hospital, it seemed too much of a coincidence that she had been taking care of each of these nine patients before they suddenly died, and they proceeded to press charges against Lucia.

The Trial and Sentencing

The allegations against Lucia involved cases from three hospitals in the immediate area, all of which had suspicious deaths occur while she was on duty and present. She was brought to trial in March 2003, and was only charged with the deaths and attempted deaths that the medical experts concluded had no natural causes. It was suggested that Lucia had poisoned each patient, resulting in cardiac arrest and death. In some cases the patients had been saved by cardiopulmonary resuscitation, but Lucia was still charged with attempted murder in these cases.

During the trial, Lucia's character was naturally brought into question. It was alleged that she had once worked as a prostitute while living in Canada and also in the Netherlands, before she became a nurse. It was also alleged that she suffered from depression, and her own brother claimed she was an avid liar and he believed she was capable of committing murder.

But what really sealed the fate of Lucia was the judiciary relying on statistical reports that showed that the probability of a nurse being on duty during each incident was 1 in 342 million. With such staggering odds, the trial only lasted five days, and at the end Lucia was found guilty of the murders and attempted murders on March 24, 2003. The sentence she received was life imprisonment, and in the Netherlands, life meant life.

The first appeal was put forward on June 18, 2004. This was rejected, and the conviction was upheld. Lucia was also sentenced to detention with psychiatric treatment, even though the criminal psychologist assigned by the state could find no evidence that she was suffering from a mental illness. The case was then presented to the Netherlands Supreme Court in March 2006, at which time it was deemed incorrect to impose a psychiatric detention at the same time as life imprisonment. Despite this, the Supreme Court returned the case back to the court in Amsterdam to reevaluate any facts that had arisen to support an appeal. Just days after the Supreme Court had made its ruling, Lucia suffered a stroke and was admitted to the prison hospital. On July 13, 2006, the Court of Appeal upheld the initial verdict and conviction, and the life sentence was given once again. This time however, the psychiatric detention was dismissed.

Doubts Emerge

Many people had begun to support Lucia, and a committee was created that continuously expressed doubts about her conviction and sentence. One of these doubts pertained to the usage of chain-link proof, wherein a person found guilty without reasonable doubt in one case is therefore guilty in subsequent cases. For Lucia, that meant that because she was found guilty of two of the murders, the court system therefore concluded she must be guilty of the others. This also means that evidence does not need to be terribly strong in all of the cases.

The two murders that were supposedly proven were based on the fact that the medical experts were unable to find the deaths were caused by natural causes. Digoxin was the drug suspected of poisoning in both of the patients, and it was supposedly detected in samples from one child by two separate laboratories. However, the methods used were not refined enough to exclude that it could have actually been a similar substance the body naturally produces. The samples were sent to another laboratory, the Strasbourg Laboratory, which used a newer method that tests for sensitivity and high specificity, meaning the analysis was more delicate. They found that there was no evidence to support the presence of digoxin, and so the allegation of death by poisoning with this drug was not conclusive.

For the other child, it was surmised that the overdose could have been due to a faulty prescription. In both cases, there were no clear signs as to how Lucia was even able to administer the digoxin. There was even evidence thrown out by the prosecution that proved Lucia wasn't in the room with one of the patients when they died. If this had been put forward during the trial, the whole synopsis of Lucia being the only one present on each occasion would have been brought into speculation and doubt.

Initially Lucia had been charged with thirteen counts of murder and medical emergencies, but the defense was able to prove that Lucia had not been present in many of these cases. At one point, she had even been away on leave, and it was simply an administrative error that put her there at the wrong time. Up until the last death that triggered the investigation, every other death later considered to be murder had been classified as being due to natural causes. Even the last case was initially put down as a natural death until it was suggested that one nurse, Lucia, had been with each patient that had died.

During the trial, the court favored the use of statistical calculations to determine the likelihood that one particular nurse may be present during so many deaths. The calculation that the chances were as low as 1 in 342 million more or less sealed Lucia's fate, as that was the statistic the court used to determine her guilt. It was later determined that the figure was closer to 1 in 25 that a nurse would be present during a spate of hospital deaths. When you consider a nurse's shifts, how often they are at the hospital, the type of wards they work in, and the size of the hospital itself, it is more than possible for one nurse to be with a number of patients as they die.

Reopening of the Case

Cases are generally not reopened in the Dutch legal system unless a new fact is presented. They don't consider different interpretations of old facts by experts. However, Tom Derksen and Metta de Noo submitted their research to the Posthumous II Commission, which looks at certain closed cases and checks for errors by the police and any misunderstanding of scientific and medical evidence. Derksen declared the medical experts had not been given all of the relevant information when questioned about the possibility of natural causes leading to the deaths. He also showed that the Strasbourg Laboratory had found there was no indication of digoxin poisoning, and that initial results were due to poor methods and techniques. The Commission agreed to look at the case and assigned three men from their group to investigate whether there had been other unexplained deaths when Lucia wasn't present, if all relevant information was given to the expert witnesses, and if scientific knowledge now altered the question regarding digoxin.

The Commission released their report in October 2007, recommending that the case be reopened due to the apparent tunnel vision of the investigators in the beginning. Also, with the last alleged victim, natural causes could no longer be ruled out, and in April 2008 Lucia was released from prison for three months. She would remain free from prison throughout the investigation and appeal process.

After months of investigation and hearings, the appeal hearing finally came to an end on March 17, 2010. It had been determined that none of the deaths were caused by deliberate action and that they were either due to natural causes, wrong treatments, poor diagnosing, or inadequate hospital management. The public prosecution made a formal request to the court to change the verdict to not guilty. The court agreed and delivered the verdict on April 14, 2010.

Justice Miscarried

Though there have been many cases of innocent people found guilty and imprisoned or even put to death in some countries, the case of Lucia de Berk was perhaps one of the worst, because there was never any evidence that a crime had even been committed. It was all based on supposition, coincidence, and failure to understand science. Lucia spent more than six years in jail, suffered a stroke, and had everything about her personal and professional life brought into question, not only in court but also in the media.

It is true that Lucia received financial compensation for the wrongful conviction and imprisonment, but the figure has never been made public. However, for someone who effectively lost six years of their life, money is probably little reward. The whole judicial process took a tremendous toll physically and mentally on a woman who was doing the job she loved, taking care of others. To be accused and convicted of such a terrible thing, and to be labelled an 'angel of death' must have been absolutely soul destroying. Yet, she continued to fight for her innocence, along with a barrage of supporters. Aside from the effect on Lucia, the families of the alleged victims must also have felt this miscarriage of justice, for they were led to believe their loved ones had been murdered for nine years. They too, like Lucia, were victims of the judicial system.

CHAPTER 5:

THE RICHARDSON MURDERS IN CANADA

The story behind the tragic murders of a family in Medicine Hat, Alberta, Canada, contains all the makings of a blockbuster movie—young love, a troubled teen, disapproving parents, alcohol and drugs, vampires and werewolves. Yes, vampires and werewolves. It will make you look twice at a person who is Goth, for all the wrong reasons. And it was a crime that would make history in Canada, as the instigator and perpetrator was none other than a 12-year-old girl and her much older boyfriend.

The Discovery of the Crime Scene

The discovery of the triple homicide of the Richardson family was made initially by a young six-year-old boy who had come over to play with the youngest member of the family, Jacob, aged 8. The little boy peered through a window to see if anyone was home, but what he saw would undoubtedly leave him with nightmares for many years to come. Lying on the floor of the basement, in clear view, were the bloodied bodies of two adults who weren't moving. The alarm was raised, and authorities rushed to the scene.

On entering the house, they found Marc Richardson, 42, and his wife Debra, 48, dead on the floor. It was obvious they had suffered numerous stab wounds, and authorities continued their search through the house to see if there were any further victims. Upstairs, the small body of Jacob was found with his throat cut. Those who knew the family immediately became concerned about the whereabouts and safety of the fourth member of the Richardson family, their daughter Jasmine.

The body of Marc contained more than twenty-four stab wounds, including nine in his back. His wife Debra had been stabbed at least twelve times, and their young son had a gaping wound in his throat. Bloody handprints and smears were found throughout the basement on the walls, and there was still no sign of Jasmine. The search was now on for Jasmine, for fear she had been abducted or murdered elsewhere.

A Shocking Suspect

The day after the discovery of the murdered Richardson family members, Jasmine was finally located in Leader, Saskatchewan, around 81 miles away from Medicine Hat. With her was her boyfriend, Jeremy Allan Steinke, 23, and his friend Kacy Lancaster, 19. Immediately, all three were arrested by the police and returned to Medicine Hat. During the search for evidence at the crime scene, the police had discovered several online accounts with which Jasmine and Jeremy had been talking to each other about murdering her parents, so they knew immediately who the suspects were. Kacy Lancaster was arrested and charged with being an accessory because she had driven them in her truck away from the location and had helped with disposing of evidence.

Both Jasmine and Jeremy were charged with three counts of murder, and at the tender age of twelve, Jasmine became the youngest person to ever be charged with multiple murders in Canada. Because of her age, the Youth Criminal Justice Act prevented her name from being published once she was deemed a suspect. Also under Canadian law, any suspect who is under fourteen years of age cannot be tried as an adult, and the maximum sentence that can be given is ten years. The same luck didn't apply to Jeremy, as at the age of twenty-three he was most certainly an adult and would be tried as such.

Jasmine's trial began in June 2007, and by then she had turned fourteen. The charges were three counts of first degree murder, to which she plead not guilty to all. Her trial lasted about a month, and in July she was found guilty of all counts by the jury, who had needed just three hours of deliberation. Sentencing for Jasmine took place in November of the same year, and, as expected, she was sentenced to ten years in prison. Part of her sentence required her to spend four years in a psychiatric hospital, and after the term of her full sentence, she would be placed under conditional supervision within the community for a further four and a half years. Her sentence was due to be completed in 2015, by which time she would have turned twenty-three years old.

Steinke Goes on Trial

By all accounts, Jeremy Steinke was a disturbed young man. Some men will do anything for love, and Jeremy really took this to the extreme by helping his very young girlfriend murder her family. Of course, it's not the first time this has happened, and no doubt it will happen again. At the age of twenty-three, Jeremy had not matured very much at all and had made claims that he was a vampire, a werewolf, and a Gothic. With piercings, tattoos, a love of blood, kink fetishes, and razorblades, it's no wonder alarm bells were ringing with Jasmine's parents. Unfortunately, those same alarm bells were not being heard by the authorities.

The night of the murders, Jeremy stated he had been drinking red wine and beer and had consumed a considerable amount of cocaine. He then climbed through an open window into the basement of the Richardson home and waited. Debra heard a noise downstairs and went down to check it out, and she must have been shocked to see Jeremy standing there armed with a knife. He grabbed her and started stabbing her over and over again.

Marc Richardson was the next to die. He too heard a noise and went down to the basement. While being attacked by Jeremy, Marc fought back as hard as he could, armed with nothing more than a screwdriver, but it was no use. Allegedly, as he was dying Marc asked Jeremy why he was doing this, and Jeremy explained it was what Jasmine wanted. Imagine that being the last thing a father hears. There was no doubt that Jeremy had killed the parents, but the murder of their eight-year-old son Jacob was not as clear.

While in custody, Jeremy had mistakenly had a conversation with someone he thought was another inmate but in fact was an undercover cop. Jeremy was open about the crime, claiming responsibility to the undercover cop, and it was this conversation that turned the opinion around regarding the death of young Jacob. According to Jeremy, it was Jasmine that had slit her little brother's throat and watched him die. To make it even more chilling, she allegedly showed no emotion, guilt, or remorse while doing so.

Jeremy had a pretty big mouth and made numerous statements to a variety of people about his role in the crime. He had told friends that he had "gutted her parents like fish." Right after the murders, they even went to a friend's house and had sex. And it was another friend that helped them get away from the town that night. Whether these people were afraid of Jeremy for some reason, or maybe just didn't care about what he and Jasmine had done, is disturbing.

On November 17, 2008, Jeremy's trial began in Calgary. The trial was originally going to take place in Medicine Hat, but Jeremy's legal team asked for the move so that the jury wouldn't be swayed by public knowledge at the time. It really wouldn't have made much difference, as the story of the murders had become a national news event, and the outcome would most likely have been the same regardless of where the trial took place.

Testimony included numerous statements from friends and associates, some of whom had been asked to help with the murders and declined. There were also internet and computer conversations where the two of them had openly discussed their plan to kill Jasmine's parents, including different methods of killing. Kacy Lancaster, who drove them to Saskatchewan the night of the murders, claimed she knew nothing about what they had just done. She stated she only found out after reading the newspaper, and she noted that both Jeremy and Jasmine showed no emotion about it at all. She had also noticed there was blood in Jeremy's truck, along with weapons including baseball bats and knives.

Not surprisingly, Jeremy was found guilty of first degree murder for each of the victims. On December 15, 2008, he was handed down three life sentences. They are concurrent sentences, and Jeremy will be eligible for parole after twenty-five years, in 2031.

A Lethal Romance

There were so many things wrong with this romance, it's hard to know where to begin. Jasmine and Jeremy had apparently met in the early part of 2006, with some saying the meeting happened at a punk rock concert, while others say it started as an online romance. In any case, Jeremy was twenty-three years old at the time, and Jasmine was just twelve. You have to wonder what a man of that age would see in such a young girl, but they quickly became a couple.

Naturally, Jasmine's parents were totally against the relationship and had every right to be. Not only was the age difference a huge problem, but it was Jeremy's background and character that worried them the most. At one point Jeremy claimed to be a 300-year-old werewolf. An adult would see through this as nonsense, but a 12-year-old child may not have the maturity to see through it. If you put yourself in Jasmine's shoes, she had a much older man interested in her, a man that seemed (to her) to be worldly and be interested in the same dark interests as herself. He told her he loved her, and he most probably did, and for a young girl, that's all she would need to hear. Don't be mistaken in thinking she was the victim, however—this girl, despite her age, knew how to manipulate her boyfriend extremely well.

Girls often go for the 'bad boy', and in the case of Jasmine and Jeremy, they thought of themselves as soulmates, lovers that would be together for ever. The only thing standing in their way (despite the obvious statutory rape law) was her parents. They were completely opposed to the relationship, and had instructed Jasmine not to see Jeremy anymore. A young teenage girl, Jasmine was adamant that she wanted to spend the rest of her life with Jeremy, and so it was her that came up with the idea of killing her parents. In her mind, that was the only way they could be together. Jeremy, being the love-sick dutiful boyfriend, agreed, and so the stage was set for what would be one of the most disturbing multiple murders ever committed in Medicine Hat.

Once both had been arrested and held in custody, they continued to communicate with each other for a long time. Their letters contained dreams and plans that one day they would run away together and get married. However, the relationship broke down and crumbled when Jeremy stated during his trial that he did not kill young Jacob and that it had been Jasmine who dealt the fatal wound. Jasmine had categorically stated that she had no part in the actual killings. She would have seen Jeremy's statement as a betrayal, and so she stopped communicating with him.

The Aftermath

Jeremy would attempt to launch an appeal, but not in 2012. He claimed it took him so long because he didn't know the system and the processes, and his defense attorney no longer wished to represent him. Normally following a murder conviction, if an appeal is to be lodged it is done so almost immediately. However, Jeremy subsequently withdrew his appeal and continues to sit in prison.

Things were very different for Jasmine. Her sentence as a minor was nothing at all like the hard time Jeremy is doing, and yet she seemed to be the main instigator of the crime. With only a ten-year sentence applicable due to her age, she completed her mandatory four years in a psychiatric facility and a further four and a half years in the community under supervision. Now twenty-two years of age, Jasmine is attending college and living with only minimum conditions as imposed by the courts. It is almost as though she got away with everything, even though it was her idea. If she had been a little bit older when the crimes were committed, things would have been very different for her.

CHAPTER 6:

THE GOOD HART MURDERS

The upper-middle-class Robison family from Detroit was vacationing at their cabin in Lake Michigan, north of Good Hart, when they met a horrific fate. It was 1968, and the family had decided to spend their whole summer at the cabin, a secluded spot surrounded by dense woods and tall trees. It was almost impossible to see the cabin from the road, which would lead investigators to believe the crime was committed by someone who knew the family and knew they would be there.

Family on Vacation

The Robison family consisted of Richard, 42, his wife Shirley, and their four children, Richie, 19, Gary, 17, Randy, 12, and Susan, aged 7. Richard owned and operated a small advertising agency called R.C. Robison & Associates and also published a magazine called Impresario. His wife of twenty years, Shirley, took good care of the home and the family, and they all attended church regularly. The children were all thought of as good students and well-mannered young people, with the eldest son Richie attending university at the time of the murders.

The family decided to go on vacation from their home in Lathrup Village, Michigan, to their cabin they had named Summerset, which was nestled on the banks of Lake Michigan near Good Hart. The family was considered to be well off, with Richard owning his company, as well as owning and piloting his own plane, and the adults attending theater regularly. They were good, honest folk who didn't gamble, drink, smoke, or get involved in any other activities deemed risky or of poor social status.

On July 22, 1968, a nearby neighbor had called the caretaker of the area, Monnie Bliss, claiming she was trying to hold a bridge game in her home, and there was an awful smell coming from the Robison's cabin. Many people were aware that the Robison's were meant to be going away at some time, so the caretaker wondered if an animal had crawled into the home and died, so he went to investigate. He knocked on the door but received no answer. Bliss opened the door, and the sight that greeted him made him alert the authorities immediately.

A Horrific Crime Scene

The local deputies converged on the scene and braced themselves for what they had been told was inside the cabin. On entering, they encountered masses of dead flies on the floor and pools of blood that had congealed. The bodies were noticed immediately, and all seemed to be dressed as though they were going out somewhere on their last day alive. There was even a suitcase partially packed sitting on one of the beds. It was estimated that the family had been dead for about four weeks, given the extent of the decomposition, and the local hospital refused to take them due to their state. Ludicrously, a chicken coop at a nearby fairground was used as a temporary morgue where the autopsies could be completed.

There was a difference with how Shirley Robison was left after she had been murdered. Her skirt had been pushed up and her underwear was down around her ankles. It was not certain if she had been raped, as the medical examiner failed to find any evidence as such, but the way her body was posed does indicate some sort of sexual assault had occurred. At the time of the murder, Shirley had been wearing a sanitary napkin, and it had seven perforations in it, almost like stab wounds. This could also indicate a sexual attack had occurred.

All of the victims had been shot, and both Richard and young Susan had also been bludgeoned with a hammer. Why that was necessary is not known. Shooting a child is one thing, but to strike her with a hammer is macabre. The date of death was eventually put down as Tuesday afternoon or evening on June 25, 1968. During the crime scene investigation, gas masks had to be worn to deal with the horrific odor from the decaying bodies. The Emmet County prosecutor at the time, Wayne Richard Smith, commented that the suit he wore that day was never worn again. He ended up burning it.

Evidence and Theories

From what the crime scene showed, the killer had approached the house around twilight and initially fired shots into the living room using a .22 caliber rifle. Richard had been sitting in an easy chair and was struck in the chest. The other family members would have been stunned, so it was easy for the killer to shoot them as he burst in through the front door. Randy, Shirley, and Susan were shot as he entered, and as Richie and Gary raced from the room to the back bedroom to retrieve a gun from the closet, they too were shot and killed. For some unknown reason, the killer then went back to Susan and struck her in the head with a hammer. To ensure they were all finished off, each member of the Robison family was then shot one more time in the head.

With the amount of gunfire that took place inside the cabin, it's a wonder nobody raised the alarm. But those that lived the closest were out at the time, and those who did hear gunshots and shouting assumed that because it was still quite light outside perhaps the Robison's were out by the beach shooting gulls.

As the murderer was leaving the house, he dragged Richard, Randy, and Susan into the hallway and put a blanket over Shirley. The killer then closed all of the curtains and turned up the heat before locking the door on his way out. The last thing he did at the scene was to cover a broken window with cardboard and tape a note to it that said 'will be back—Robison'. Presumably, this was to make anyone think the family was simply away for a day or two, giving the killer enough time to make his escape without being noticed in the vicinity.

There were many theories tossed about during the investigation into these murders. Some of the local residents were concerned there was a random madman on the loose, and they feared for their own safety. At the time there was a serial killer by the name of John Norman Collins, aka the 'co-ed killer,' operating in the area, but his modus operandi was far different, so it was not likely to be him. Nevertheless, he came under suspicion simply because he was a murderer acting locally.

The Suspects

Richard Robison

The first direction the police looked was towards Richard and his business and personal life. Often when a family is assassinated in such a way, it is the act of someone close to one of the victims. On looking into Richard's life, investigators found that he wasn't really the man everyone thought he was. They uncovered the secret that he had several affairs during his marriage to Shirley. Could this then be the work of a jealous lover or an irate husband? He also liked to bring his secretary into his office and ask her to lift her skirt so he could look at her legs. Although there was no intercourse with the secretaries, he would touch and fondle them for up to an hour at a time.

The wonderful businessman, deemed a pillar of society, had also done some very suspicious business dealings, resulting in some clients being swindled by up to $50,000. Over a three year period, he would bill the client for advertisements he either didn't pay for or didn't even run. Richard would also create and publish full-page ads for airlines without asking for their permission so that his magazine would look as though it was more successful than it actually was.

Richard had come up with a scheme to create giant computerized warehouses at airports internationally. He was looking to raise $100 million from a group of investors referred to as the 'Superior Table'. He claimed this group was a global organization dedicated to bringing peace and unity among all countries. The chairman of the group was allegedly a man named Roebert. Robison even wore a St. Christopher medal with an inscription from Roebert which read: 'Richard—to my chosen son and heir —God bless you—Roebert.' Before the Robison family left for their ill-fated vacation, Richard had been dropping hints around that he was expecting a visit from a 'Mr. Roberts' while they would be at the cabin to talk about a multi-million dollar deal. However, nobody by that name ever flew in through the nearest airport, and detectives wondered if Mr. Roberts and Roebert were the same man, or if they even ever existed.

Organized Crime

There was a large possibility that there was an organized crime link to the murders for a variety of reasons. First, one of Richard's former secretaries went on to marry a powerful and very rich manufacturing tycoon who was rumored to have ties with organized crime in Cleveland. Around the same time as the murders, the secretary had suffered a miscarriage, and there were that the baby was Robison's and not her husbands after all.

As mentioned before, Richard had swindled a number of families out of substantial amounts of money. One of those families was allegedly associated with organized crime, so the detectives had to consider the murders were a hit as payback. Also, one of the weapons used in the murders, the AR-7, was very popular among the Mafia hit men at that time. Another rumor was that Robison was behind in his payments to the mob, and if he had paid when he was supposed to, they would still be alive.

Bloxom, Brock, and Matthews

Early in 1970, an inmate at Leavenworth prison in Kansas told a story to the detectives that implicated himself and two other men in the murders of the Robison's. The inmate was Alexander Bloxom, referred to as a career criminal, who had been living in a halfway house with a man named Mark Warren Brock back in 1968. He had driven Brock to a restaurant in Flint for a meeting with a man he thought was called 'Scollata'. Afterwards, Brock traveled to Toledo and collected some weapons. He then headed north with another man named Robert Matthews. Bloxom had stayed behind because he was told there weren't any colored people in Good Hart. Two days after the murders, Brock returned.

Bloxom had the ability to recall a lot of detail. He perfectly described Richard Robison's briefcase, which he claimed Brock returned home with and destroyed later. He also had in his possession a black suitcase with guns inside, among other items, including a photograph of the Robison's and cancelled checks. These items were to be kept for future blackmail purposes, and Bloxom was instructed to get rid of the suitcase at a salvage yard in Alabama. The envelope was hidden at a relative's home.

According to Bloxom, Brock had told him they went to the cabin and knocked on the door, and he then faked having a heart attack. He lay down on the floor, and as Richard tried to help him, Matthews came in to the cabin and opened fire. He also said the wife was shot first, then one of the children who had tried to run, and then they just killed them all.

Brock was in prison when Bloxom's story came out, and he actually verified almost every detail of the story. He even admitted he wouldn't be opposed to carrying out a murder for the right price, but he was adamant he did not murder the Robison family. The three men—Bloxom, Brock and Matthews—

were given polygraph tests to confirm or rule out their story. Surprisingly, Matthews passed his test. Bloxom was eager to do his test, but he ended up failing it. Brock flat out refused to take a polygraph test. Without definite corroboration or evidence, the theory that Brock and Matthews had killed the Robison's was inconclusive, so none of the men were charged.

Monnie Bliss the Caretaker

Many of the locals in the area pointed the finger at Monnie Bliss as being the culprit. His father and he had actually built the homes in the area, including the Robison cabin, and it was afterwards that Bliss took up residency as the main caretaker. Who better to do repairs on the cabins than the very man himself who built them? Despite his handyman skills, Bliss was known to have a short temper and would often be found talking to himself. Some of the locals were even afraid of Bliss, thinking he was a bit odd.

So why would Bliss murder the Robison's? It turns out, when his 18-year-old son was killed in a motorcycle accident while riding drunk, Bliss held the Robison family accountable. Apparently, his son had been with the older Robison boys that same day. To make matters worse, the day before the funeral, Richard had visited the family to offer his condolences and explain they would be unable to attend the funeral. That might not have been so bad, except that Richard then gave his wife just $20 towards flowers, which Bliss found insulting. It was the very next night the family was murdered.

Some investigators felt that the female victims were subject to overkill and were therefore the target of revenge. The use of a hammer on Susan also brought suspicion on Bliss, as he was a builder by trade, so naturally would own a hammer. There was even a rumor that his hammer had gone missing from his toolbox. However, the police considered this information to be the result of locals having a chat over a beer and speculating, rather than fact, and Bliss was cleared as a suspect. His behavior continued to be more and more bizarre, and at times he was heard to say he thought the Robison's had it coming. In some cases, he claimed he had killed the family during his semi-crazy ramblings.

The Co-Ed Killer

The co-ed killer was otherwise known as John Norman Collins, a man who was charged with one murder but suspected of up to fifteen more. He operated in California and Michigan between 1967 and 1969, and his victims were young women. His murderous spree came to an end when his uncle, a state police corporal, became suspicious. Collins had actually used his uncle's house to murder an 18-year-old woman named Karen Sue Beineman, a student at the same university Collins attended. Ironically, another fellow student at the East Michigan University was none other than Richie Robison.

Stories came about that Richie and Collins were in the same fraternity there and would therefore have known each other. Others claimed that the two had met during orientation at the university, and Collins could have visited Richie at the family cottage in Good Hart where the murders eventually took place. This would show that Collins knew where the secluded cabin was, an important factor in investigating the crime. Police never considered Collins a strong suspect, but they kept him in the back of their minds as a potential lead.

Collins adamantly denies taking any part in the murders of the Robison family. He is serving a life sentence for the murder of Karen Beineman and has stated that being convicted of one murder is one thing, but to be labelled for things he hadn't done was unfair. It's important to remember, the other murders he was suspected of committing have never been proven to be the work of Collins.

Joseph R. Scolaro – Embezzler?

Within two weeks of the investigation following the discovery of the Robison bodies, the police had a very firm suspect in mind. Joseph Scolaro was an employee of Richard's, and he had disappeared for more than twelve hours on the day of the murders. He had provided alibis for that time period, though none of them were valid. He had also recently purchased guns, the same as the ones used to commit the murders, as determined by forensic ballistic experts. These included a .25-caliber Jet-Fire automatic Beretta pistol and a .22-caliber AR-7 ArmaLite semi-automatic rifle. Forensics compared the four .22-caliber shells found at the cabin with those that had been fired by Scolaro at his family firing range, and they were found to be a match. In his defense, Scolaro claimed he had given the rifle away to someone, but a neighbor stated to police he had seen the gun at Scolaro's house not long before the murders.

Scolaro also claimed to have given away the .25-caliber pistol, and when questioned he provided a second pistol of the same caliber to the police that he had purchased at the same time as the other ones. At the crime scene were found some SAKO .25-caliber cartridges, which are a rare brand of ammunition produced in Finland. This particular ammunition is only sold during a short and specific time period each year, and one of the purchasers listed in Michigan was Scolaro. Police were able to determine that Scolaro's claims of giving away the guns were untrue, and Scolaro was unable to prove otherwise.

During their investigation, a forensic accountant was brought in to analyze the financial affairs of the Robison's and the advertising company and the magazine Richard owned. It was found that over $60,000 seemed to be missing from the company accounts. Scolaro had been left in charge of both companies for the summer while the Robison's were on vacation, and this implicated Scolaro as the killer due to embezzlement and his trying to hide his financial crime.

Despite all of this, the prosecutor was unwilling to bring charges against Scolaro without more evidence. The fact that there were no fingerprints at the crime scene and that the guns had gone missing made it difficult to prove Scolaro was ever there. Further doubts arose about the amount of time it would take Scolaro to travel from Detroit to Good Hart, kill the Robison's, and return back to Detroit. The trip one way takes between five and six hours to complete as it is, and with witnesses claim they heard gunshots around 9pm, it would be hard to comprehend how Scolaro got there and back within the twelve hours he was apparently missing. Scolaro's wife stated he was home with her by 11 p.m. that night, so if they were killed at 9 p.m., there was no possible way he could be home with his wife by then.

Furthermore, although Scolaro may have been embezzling money from his employer, it is a big jump to then turn around and murder an entire family, especially considering the brutality shown to the female victims. White-collar criminals tend to stay just that—financial fraud is quite different than physical and violent crime. Besides, although $60,000 might seem a lot to many people, it's not really the kind of figure you go on a murderous rampage for, even if you are terrified of getting caught. Unless of course the embezzlement amount was much larger. On the morning of the murders, Richard called the bank to check if a deposit he was expecting had been made, to the value of $200,000. It hadn't, so Richard immediately tried to contact Scolaro, who also had access to the account. Richard made multiple attempts to get hold of Scolaro throughout the day without any success. Back in the office, Scolaro had been told Richard was trying to get hold of him, and instead of calling him back, he just left and disappeared for the rest of the day.

Another theory was that Scolaro paid someone else to do the hit for him, which would fit in with Bloxom's story (remember the name he recalled—Scollata—is very similar). Perhaps Scolaro provided the guns, the ammunition, directions to the cabin, and could have even paid for the hit using some of the money he stole. The investigators thought there was enough evidence and information to press charges. In 1973, the prosecutor's office was on the right path to being able to file murder conspiracy charges, and Scolaro got wind of it. Shortly after, Scolaro was found dead in his office chair from a self-inflicted gunshot wound. He left a note for his mother in which he that although he was a liar, a phony and a cheat, he did not have anything to do with the murders. To others, despite what the note said, his suicide was an indication of guilt, but we'll really never know.

Nothing Resolved....Yet

To date, there has been no resolution in this multiple murder case. In 2013, detectives were still keeping an eye on the open case, and they have continued to investigate as the years have passed on. Although there have been many theories and multiple suspects, they have never been able to just narrow it down to one. With so many people now passed on, a lot of information will have died with them, so it becomes even more complicated as time passes. However, they are not giving up. They are praying for some kind of miracle, that someone will confess or at least come forward with specific information, so they can finally serve justice on the killer or killers of the Robison family.

CHAPTER 7:

BESLANOWITCH – THE MURDER OF A TEEN PROSTITUTE

The killing of prostitutes is nothing new. They have been a particularly popular victim among serial killers due to their transient and high-risk lifestyle. Many of the women working the streets have few friends and very little family contact, and they can be missing for days or even weeks and months before anyone realizes they are missing. This delay is a real asset for a killer, as the more time passes, the less likely the chance is that he will be identified. It's saddening to think that these women are preyed upon simply because their lives have taken a turn for the worse. Drug addiction, abuse, alcoholism, and homelessness are all factors associated with many women who end up as prostitutes. Just because they are desperate, and even though their families may not be in touch as much, they are still human beings—someone's daughter, sister, mother, girlfriend or grandchild. They are still loved.

The Life of Krystal Beslanowitch

The body found on the banks of the Provo River near Midway, Utah, on December 15, 1995, was identified as Krystal Beslanowitch. She had grown up in Spokane, and had fallen by the wayside at the young age of fifteen years. By then, she was already involved in drugs and prostitution. Her mother has said that every time Krystal came back home, she always accepted her back. It seemed that Krystal just wasn't interested in living a normal life, despite the love and support she got at home.

Her stepfather claimed that Krystal had started selling her body much younger, at the age of twelve years old, and he also claimed she had given birth to a baby that was subsequently taken from her. He felt sorry for Krystal and believed she never really stood a chance in life. In July 1995, Krystal and her boyfriend decided to move away, and they moved to Utah. Krystal had been in trouble with the law on numerous occasions while in Spokane. The charges included prostitution, assault, drug violations, and auto theft. Perhaps they thought it was time to try their luck in a different city.

One night Krystal headed out to go to a convenience store and she never came back. Her boyfriend waited two days before he reported her missing. It's not known why he waited so long. Perhaps she had done it before and always returned. What made him more concerned was that another prostitute who had worked the same area as Krystal, west North Temple, had been murdered that November, just a month earlier.

Cold on the River Bank

Krystal went missing on a Friday, and her body was found the next day by two ranchers. They had been traveling down a country road that was quite isolated and noticed the body on the banks of the river. They notified the authorities immediately, and local law enforcement headed to the crime scene.

Krystal's body was completely nude, and it was obvious to those who saw her that she had suffered numerous traumatic blows to the head and face. The medical examiner would later confirm she had been struck at least eight or nine times with a large rock. She was just seventeen years old at the time of her death, which made it even more intolerable for the hard-nosed detectives. In fact, a sheriff's deputy named Todd Bonner was haunted by the case throughout his entire career. Once they had identified Krystal, they next had to try to find a suspect.

It wasn't going to be an easy task, and there seemed to be no leads whatsoever. It was difficult to say whether she had been murdered by a client while she was working as a prostitute or whether she was the victim of circumstance and just happened to cross paths with the wrong person at the wrong time. One thing is for sure; her boyfriend was ruled out very early on in the investigation.

During the autopsy, forensic evidence was obtained from underneath her fingernails, and forensic experts also collected evidence from the alleged murder weapon, the large rocks that had been used to bash in her head. However, forensic science wasn't as advanced back then, and it lead nowhere.

Reopening of the Case

In 2008, two detectives were assigned to reopen the case with the hopes of a breakthrough using new forensic technology. The detectives worked full time on the case, and forensic scientists were able to extract more DNA from the rocks found with her body. The DNA was run through the CODIS database and the detectives waited for a match.

The main focus of reopening the case was to further explore the forensic evidence found at the scene of the crime. Rather than re-interviewing people or revisiting the scene, attention was turned to science, and the numerous advances that had occurred. Now it was possible to get a DNA profile from a much smaller sample, and it was this that lead the police straight to the murderer.

DNA Points the Finger

All their wishes came through in January 2009, when CODIS returned a DNA match. The suspect's name was Joseph Michael Simpson, a 46-year-old man who had already served time in prison for murder back in the 1980s. He had lived in Clearfield for a time, and in 2009 was residing in Sarasota County, Florida.

The match encouraged the team to further analyze other forensic evidence from the crime scene, and this came back even stronger as belonging to Simpson. By now Todd Bonner was the Wasatch Country Sherriff, and although he wasn't heavily involved in the case, he kept his hand in it, so he was aware of what was going on at all times. Despite having the DNA match, it was decided that they needed more biological evidence from Simpson. Bonner and another detective set off to find Simpson.

They needed a fresh sample of Simpson's DNA, so they tracked him down and followed him. On August 25, 2013, they managed to follow him into a store, a smoke shop, and when he finished smoking his cigarette, Bonner grabbed it. Now they had the DNA they needed. As expected, it was a match. Simpson was subsequently arrested at his home for the murder of Krystal, and it was Bonner who had the joy of placing him in handcuffs.

He was taken to the local jail in Sarasota to await extradition back to Utah, where he would be formally charged with the murder of Krystal. Surprisingly, Simpson didn't try to fight the extradition order and was eventually returned to Utah.

Simpson's History – It Wasn't His First Murder

At the time he was arrested by Bonner, Simpson had been living in Sarasota County for nearly fourteen years. He was unemployed and living with his parents at the age of forty-six. Before then, he had lived in Clearfield, Utah. Once in custody, more information came about regarding the background of Simpson, and it was found that he had a strong history of violence.

Back in 1987, Simpson had been arrested for stabbing a man in Clearfield. It wasn't a simple stabbing —there were thirteen knife wounds in the victim, causing his death. His trial was relatively swift, and he was found guilty of second degree murder. He would go on to serve roughly eight years for the crime and was paroled in April 1995. He had only been out of prison for a few months when he murdered his next victim, Krystal.

He seemed to favor killing methods that involved being up close and personal. First was the stabbing of his first victim, as you need to be very close to a person to stab them, especially that number of times. Then, when crushing Krystal's skull with a large rock, he needed to be positioned close to or standing over Krystal to repeatedly smash the rock against her head. This method is also perhaps the most gruesome, and shows what Simpson was really capable of.

Even while in jail awaiting trial, he gained another charge of assault against a fellow inmate. As of now, he has not been sent to trial, so it is all just a matter of waiting. Despite the gravity of the crime, the prosecution has stated that they do not intend to seek the death penalty but will go for life imprisonment. Some say this is not enough. He has killed two people now, both in an extremely violent manner, and convicted criminals have been sent to death for less horrific murders. Time will tell what the outcome will be when the trial goes ahead.

CHAPTER 8:

MURDER OR ACCIDENT?

The case of two teenage girls disappearing into the night in 1971 had plagued the families, friends and the community for decades. They were good girls who headed out for some fun and never came back. Were they murdered? Had they been abducted? Some even wondered if they had simply run away. Or was there another reason they vanished...it would be a mystery for forty-three years.

Sherri Miller and Pam Jackson Disappear

Sherri and Pam were both from Vermilion, and both were just seventeen years old and were still attending high school. Sherri was a smart girl and was living with her grandparents after her mother had remarried then moved away. She was very independent and knew what she wanted in life and what she didn't want, a good head on her shoulders. Her grandmother had been diagnosed with terminal cancer, and Sherri willingly looked after her through the spring in 1971, as well as taking care of her grandfather. It was her job to get her grandfather out of bed in the morning, fix his breakfast, and take care of the daily chores. Because of her caring nature, she ended up working after school hours at the local Dakota Hospital, which is where her friend Pam Jackson worked as well.

Sherri wanted to go into the fashion design industry and was an avid sewer. Her plan was to move to California once she had graduated from high school, along with her cousin Pam Stewart. Pam Jackson also had an interest in dress design, and the two of them had many other things in common. On the night of May 29, 1971, Sherri had invited Pam Jackson to go out with her that night, and although Pam's mother said no at first, she ended up giving in. Pam Stewart was also going to go along with the girls, but she was called out to babysit at the last minute.

The girls made a stop at the hospital to visit with Sherri's grandmother and left there around 9:30 that night. They were driving around in Sherri's grandfather's 1960 Studebaker, a solid car that ran well. They met up with some boys from school after leaving the hospital and were invited along to a party taking place at a nearby gravel pit. The girls agreed to follow the boys there.

At one point, the boys in the car ahead had made a wrong turn, and when they doubled back there was no sign of the girls and the Studebaker. At 4 a.m. the next morning, Pam Jackson's mother noticed Pam hadn't turned off the kitchen light like she normally would when she got home. She had a look in her room and discovered she wasn't home. She assumed the girls had experienced car trouble and probably stayed in town for the night with a friend.

Later that morning, Pam's parents started to call everyone they could think of to see if the girls had spent the night, but nobody had seen them. Sherri's grandmother was critical, and in fact, she died just six days after Sherri went missing. The police naturally assumed the girls had run away, but they hadn't taken any clothing, makeup (they were teenage girls after all), or even the paychecks they had received that day. There was also no way Sherri would have abandoned her grandmother when she was so gravely ill.

The suggestion was made to drag the river to see if the girls had crashed, but it was decided that the current was too swift and it wouldn't be safe. The visibility in the water was very poor, so sending down divers wouldn't have achieved anything either. Pam's father would spend days walking up and down the gravel roads and across the nearby fields looking for any signs of the girls. Sherri's father would sit at the local police department looking at photo after photo of unidentified deceased girls, and he checked her social security to see if it was being used by anyone, but it wasn't. The girls had vanished into thin air.

A False Accusation

How a man named David Lykken came to be accused of murdering both Sherri and Pam is quite extraordinary. When questioned, he was already serving 225 years in prison for rape and kidnapping. With no bodies, no forensic evidence, and no witness statements it's hard to believe he was considered for the alleged crime in the first place.

However, Lykken had a very dark history and was in the area of Vermillion at the time the two girls disappeared. The case was handed on to the newly-formed cold case unit in 2004, and was one of the first cases investigated. The fact that Lykken had lived close to the gravel pit where the party was meant to take place that night, and because he had a history of violence towards women, it was deemed he needed to be investigated further.

While going back over the previous records and documents, there was one piece of information gathered back in 1971 that further convinced the investigators to look at Lykken. A neighbor of Pam Jackson's family had reported that she had overheard a party line phone conversation a month before the girls disappeared. It was reportedly a conversation between Pam Jackson and a man named David. The neighbor believed David was a student at the University of South Dakota, but wasn't sure.

They began to question Lykken's victims to try and find out as much information as they could about the crimes he had committed. They also spoke to his younger sister, who claimed he was often violent and threatening. She even recalled an incident in which David told her to drive, and he climbed into the back of the car and raped a female passenger. According to his sister, David had taken the same school bus with Sherri, and he knew both Sherri and Pam through the church.

His sister recalled a time shortly after the disappearances when her family was digging large pits on their farm and creating a large fire. Her parents had often tried to cover for David when he got into trouble, but he still had a lot of anger towards them. The sister didn't know why this was, but she had been told once it was something to do with a girl buried on the farm. At this point in time, she was unaware the cold case team were interviewing her about Sherri and Pam.

Some of the information given by his sister was clearly not true. When asked if she had seen a car on the farm and was shown pictures of different models of Studebaker, she identified the same model Sherri had been driving that night. When asked if she saw any bodies, she claimed she saw Sherri slumped over the steering wheel and Pam with her head on the passenger window. It seemed she was feeding off the suggestions that were given to her instead of recalling actual facts.

With all of the information at hand, the investigators obtained a search warrant for David's possessions that were stored at his parent's farm and for the farmland itself. They dug up many areas as indicated by David's sister on a map, but nothing was found. Numerous other interviews with his sister took place, including under hypnosis, and it seemed as though she was recalling real memories.

In 2006, the investigation team received further information from an inmate named Aloysius Black Crow, who was incarcerated with Lykken. He claimed Lykken had confessed to him that he had murdered Sherri and Pam. They fitted him with a wire and asked him to go back and interview Lykken. He did so, and the audio recording captured Lykken stating he had asked the girls for a ride, and he had raped Pam and tied Sherri up for hours.

It was discovered in 2008 that the tape recordings were all fake, and that it was another man's voice on the tape, not Lykken's. The investigators had been sent down the wrong path—first by Lykken's own sister, then by a fraudulent inmate who was only out to gain for himself. Therefore, the charges against Lykken were dropped.

Skeletons in the Studebaker

In September 2013, the forty-three-year mystery surrounding the disappearance of Sherri Miller and Pam Jackson was finally solved. A fisherman at Brule Creek noticed wheels underneath the bridge while the water levels were low and notified the authorities. On investigation, they discovered that it was the 1960 Studebaker Lark that Sherri had been driving that night.

Inside the car were the skeletal remains of two females who would later be identified as Sherri and Pam. Their identities were confirmed through the use of DNA, and there were a number of personal items found inside the car that belonged to the girls. On examination of the bodies, it was determined that there were no signs of injuries that would indicate foul play or homicide. Instead, the girls had simply run off the road and vanished into the murky depths of the creek.

Despite the area being searched multiple times following the disappearance, the car could not be seen due to higher water levels. Tragically, Pam's father had passed away just five days before the car wreck was discovered. Although it is still a terrible tragedy that the girls were found deceased, it at last puts to rest all of the suspicions, accusations, theories, and what ifs that have plagued the families and the community for nearly fifty years.

CHAPTER 9:

WHEN SUICIDE IS MURDER

It's not always easy to tell the difference between a suicide and a murder, and sometimes information comes to light much later on that further clarifies the difference between the two. The case of Pamela Shelly is one such case. At first, it was considered a suicide by the authorities, but thanks to a true crime television program many years later, a man was subsequently caught and put behind bars for her murder.

The Death of Pamela Shelly

Pamela Shelly had been living with her boyfriend Ronnie Hendrick in De Witt County, Texas, not far from where Ronnie's parents lived. Her children Kayla, 12, and Dustin, 9, were also living with Pamela and Ronnie. The rest of her family was back in Arkansas, where she had also been living before Ronnie moved her to Texas. Pamela and her kids had only been at Ronnie's for about five months, and she was planning to leave him. Ronnie was abusive, and Pamela was taking the kids and moving back to Arkansas.

January 6, 2001, Pamela had packed her belongings and sorted the children's things out and was about to leave. They were leaving in twenty minutes time when something happened that would forever change the lives of many. A gunshot was heard, and Pamela was lying on the floor of the bathroom with a bullet wound to the head. Ronnie's stepfather placed the call to 911 asking for assistance because Pamela had attempted to kill herself.

When the ambulance got there, Pamela was still breathing. They quickly loaded her onboard and headed to nearby Cuero, where the hospital was, twenty minutes away. Ronnie was in the front cab of the ambulance giving directions, as the ambulance staff had come from out of town and didn't know their way around. By the time the police arrived at the scene, the ambulance along with Pamela and Ronnie had already left.

Many years later, the emergency services people who attended the incident all stated they must have believed it was a suicide, as there was no fear about entering the house. Usually if there is a firearm incident, the ambulance staff waits at a safe distance until the police clear the scene. This wasn't considered necessary this time and is most likely because the adults that were present all stated Pamela had tried to kill herself.

Ronnie's family made sure the authorities believed Pamela was suicidal. Ronnie claimed that Pamela was happy there, but her daughter Kayla wasn't, and so she had to return to Arkansas even though she didn't want to. Ronnie believed this was the final straw for Pamela, and she took her own life. There was apparently a family history of suicide in Pamela's family, including her sister who had successfully killed herself. Therefore, it's no wonder it seemed so plausible to the investigating officers.

The autopsy performed on Pamela showed a typical suicide

gunshot, and adding to that the information given that she was suicidal and depressed, the medical examiner happily labelled the death as a suicide. The police, however, were still uneasy and requested Ronnie take a polygraph, which he agreed to do. They arranged for the test to be done on two separate occasions, but Ronnie failed to appear each time. Weeks after Pamela's death, Ronnie disappeared.

Several years later, in 2008, a new investigator, Carl Bowen, joined the county sheriff's department. The current sheriff was Jody Zavesky, and because Carl had been on the force when Pamela died, he was aware of the case and convinced Jody to take another look at it. Carl had always been bothered by the fact that Ronnie had never taken the polygraph test and had disappeared almost immediately after Pamela died. Fueled by their own determination and personal interest, Jody and Carl reopened the case.

Carl was pleasantly surprised when that summer Ronnie Hendrick was arrested and arrived at the De Witt County Jail. He had been charged with domestic abuse, having beaten up the woman he had been sharing a home with. It turned out that following Pamela's death, Ronnie had traveled to South Dakota and spent time in prison there for felony DWI, as well. All of a sudden, things started to fall into place for Carl as he realized Ronnie was a chronic alcohol abuser and woman beater.

Finally Carl was able to get Ronnie to take the polygraph test. Not surprisingly, he failed it, and when questioned by the polygraph examiner after the test, he requested legal counsel. He told four different people that he had lied about not being in the bathroom when she was shot, but that he did not pull the trigger. Originally he had claimed to be outside the house when Pamela was shot. Things were getting more and more suspicious.

Television Steps In

Carl discovered there was a television program looking for cold cases they could work on and help solve for a new television show called Cold Justice. Although hesitant at first, it was agreed by the higher authorities that the case of Pamela Shelly could be put forward as a possible case for the program. The producers of the show jumped at the chance right away. The main investigators in the program were former Harris County ADA Kelly Siegler and a former crime scene investigator, Yolanda McClary, from Las Vegas.

The team tends to focus on police departments that are understaffed, where their expertise can be used more effectively. They arrived in June and set to work. With them came the opportunity to have access to high-tech scientific evidence results with a remarkably quick turnaround. Immediately the gun was sent for DNA analysis. Unfortunately, this did not produce the results they wanted or needed.

Next, they took a look at Pamela's medical history and noted there had never been any issue with depression or any other form of mental illness, which completely undermined Ronnie's story. They were able to cross off any information that was no longer relevant or had been disproved, while at the same time gathering new information through witness interviews, crime scene reenactments, and reanalyzing all the previous data that had been gathered. When they presented the case and new evidence, the DA took his time deciding whether or not to proceed.

The final piece of the puzzle that persuaded the DA was an interview conducted by Carl with Pamela's ex-husband Jessie, who was incarcerated in a prison in Texas. According to Jessie, he had a phone conversation the same day Pamela was shot, reconfirming that she and the children were moving back to Arkansas. He also claimed that he and Pam were going to reunite and get back together. During the conversation, Ronnie had grabbed the phone and told Jessie the only way she was going back to Arkansas was in a box. To see if he was being deceptive with his story, Jessie was given a polygraph and passed.

Ronnie Hendrick

In November 2012, Ronnie was indicted for murder. He was set to go to trial in September 2013. Unfortunately, Cold Justice had scheduled the screening of the episode about Pam just six days before the trial was due to begin. Carl contacted the producers and asked if the date could be changed, but they refused. The concern was that if the local people watched the show, they would be useless as a jury. Sure enough, when jury selection came around, so many had seen it and already formed an opinion regarding his guilt that they could not be used as jury members, so a mistrial was called.

Another date was set for the trial, which was to be in June 2014. Although what people had seen on the program may have worn off by then, there was still the chance that a jury could be difficult to select. The DA decided to use that to his advantage and had a meeting with Ronnie's attorney. When it was pointed out that every person who had watched the Cold Justice episode was likely to believe Ronnie was guilty, then the jury was going to be the same. Therefore, it was likely he would be found guilty even if a jury could be selected. The next day, Ronnie pled guilty to murder and was sentenced to twenty-two years in prison.

CHAPTER 10:

SNATCHED FROM THE SNOW

The story of Maria Ridulph is a tragic tale and one of innocence lost that would affect not only her family, but her community. It would also greatly affect a friend, who had been with her that night and witnessed the abduction, for the rest of her life. Two little girls innocently playing in the snow outside the house were ripped apart by a real life boogeyman who swept in and swept out, carrying little Maria away with him.

The Disappearance of Maria Ridulph

Maria was one of four children born to parents Michael and Frances, and they lived in Sycamore, Illinois. Most of the adults in the area worked on local farms, but Michael worked at a factory, one of the few that existed there at that time. Frances was a homemaker, taking care of the family and the home, and they seemed to have a good life.

It had started snowing on the evening of December 3, 1957, and Maria begged her parents to let her go out and play in the snow with her friend Kathy Sigman. Although it was dark out, her parents said yes, and after dinner they went outside near Maria's home and were playing a game they called 'duck the cars', where they ran back and forth avoiding the headlights of cars coming down the street. In that era it wasn't considered dangerous to let the kids out at night, as it was a fairly innocent time, a time when murders and violent crimes were not common at all.

While they were out playing, Kathy stated a man had approached them who said his name was Johnny. He told them he was twenty-four years old and had no wife, and he offered Maria a piggyback ride. She went back to her house and retrieved her favorite doll to show the stranger, as it was her prized possession. When she returned, Kathy went back to her own house to get her mittens because it was so cold. When Kathy came back, both Maria and the stranger were gone.

Unable to find Maria, Kathy went to her parent's house to tell them she couldn't find her. Maria's parents assumed she was hiding somewhere and sent their 11-year-old son out to find her. When he had no luck, the parents then called the police. Within an hour, the police had arrived along with armed civilians to search the town. They could find no trace of the little girl or the man who she had last been seen with.

Within two days of her disappearance, the FBI was called in due to the possibility Maria had been kidnapped and taken across state lines. Numerous people had seen the two girls playing together that night, but nobody had seen the stranger with them up until 6:30 p.m. They therefore believed this stranger, 'Johnny', had approached Maria and Kathy after that time, and that Maria had been taken somewhere between 6:45 and 7:00 p.m.

Because Kathy had been the only one to see Johnny, she was placed in protective custody in case he returned to take her or harm her. She was shown photos of possible suspects or those who had been convicted before to see if she could identify the man who called himself Johnny, but she could not. She was also asked to look at a lineup of suspects, and she pointed out a man named Thomas Joseph Rivard. However, Rivard had a tight alibi and couldn't have been the man they were looking for. He had only been placed in the lineup to fill up the numbers.

A Tragic Discovery

Near Woodbine, Illinois, some 100 miles away from Sycamore, two tourists were searching a wooded area looking for mushrooms on April 26, 1958. What they found was the skeletal remains of a young child. The only clothing present was a shirt, socks, and undershirt, and the tiny body was beneath a tree that had partially fallen over. The state of decomposition indicated the body had been there for months, and it was later identified as Maria through dental records. The rest of the clothing she had been wearing the night she disappeared was nowhere to be seen.

Photographs of the crime scene were not taken, as the coroner didn't want the media to get hold of them, particularly because the body was that of a child. As the body was found within the state, the FBI stepped back and left the case with the local and state police to investigate. The autopsy done at the time showed no indication of the manner of death. This was apparently due to the level of decomposition, which many years later would be handled in a different manner.

Prime Suspect Right From the Start – Was Tessier Johnny?

A young man who was considered a suspect right from the beginning was John Tessier. Originally from Ireland, he had moved to Sycamore after World War II ended with his British mother and American stepfather. Before his mother's remarriage, John's surname had been Cherry, and he would still use it from time to time.

The family home was just around the corner from the Ridulph's, and at the time John was eighteen years old and planning on joining the Air Force. During the initial search and investigation into Maria's disappearance, investigators had visited John's home and spoken to his mother. She claimed John had been home all night, whereas his sisters would later testify this wasn't true. The investigators had received a tip regarding John, and it was speculated that it may have come from a resident or John's parents themselves, trying to clear their boy's name since he had the same name as Johnny and his physical description was a match.

The next statement John made was that he had been in Rockford the night in question enlisting in the Air Force, which completely contradicted what his mother had said previously. He claimed he had called his parents from Rockford to get a ride home, as he had left his car back at the house. There was a telephone record of a collect call being made that night at 6:57 p.m. by a John Tessier. He then met with recruiting officers to drop off some paperwork, and they confirmed to the authorities that this occurred at around 7:15 p.m. that night.

Despite this, an officer wasn't convinced and asked Tessier to take a polygraph test, which he complied with and passed. Because his alibi seemed to be truthful and he had passed the polygraph, he was released and taken off the list of suspects. Of note, Kathy Sigman was never asked to identify John or look at his photograph. The following day, John left for training at the Air Force Base.

John was to complete thirteen years in the Air Force, and he obtained the rank of captain before then undertaking study to become a police officer. He worked as an officer in Lacy, Olympia, then moved to Milton, Washington. Trouble would find him in Washington in 1982 in the form of a 15-year-old runaway named Michelle Weinman and her friend. John had taken the girls in, and not long after, Michelle filed a complaint that John had fondled her and performed oral sex. He was charged with felony statutory rape and discharged from the police force. He negotiated a plea deal and pled guilty to communication with a minor for immoral purposes, which is a misdemeanor instead of a felony. John would later change his name to Jack Daniel McCullough, supposedly to honor his deceased mother.

A Mother's Deathbed Confession

In 2008, John Tessier's half-sister Janet provided new information that led to the case being reopened. She made a startling revelation that on her mother's deathbed she had stated the following: "Those two little girls, and the one that disappeared, John did it. John did it and you have to tell someone." Janet immediately assumed her mother was talking about the murder of Maria Ridulph and had been told by her elder sisters that their mother had lied to the police that night about John's whereabouts. Another of the half-sisters, Mary, was also there when their mother made the statement about John being guilty, but she only heard the words 'he did it'. Nevertheless, she also assumed it was to do with the Maria Ridulph case. At the time of their mother's death, John was not involved in the family, having previously molested a younger half-sister and threatened Janet with a gun. He wasn't even allowed to come to his mother's funeral.

Janet had made numerous attempts since her mother's death to get the Sycamore police and the FBI to consider her mother's statement. She eventually sent an email to the Illinois State Police tip line, and it was handed to the cold case unit to investigate. All of John's sisters had suspected him of being the murderer. The investigators were able to create a different timeline showing that John did have time to drive to Rockford after snatching Maria and making the phone call to his parents and meeting with the recruitment officers. This shed a whole new light on his so-called alibi.

Finally, Kathy Sigman, Maria's friend who had been there that dreadful night, was shown a photograph of John as he was back then. She immediately identified him as the stranger, 'Johnny', who had disappeared with Maria. More and more evidence was stacking up against John, as witnesses recalled new information and other witnesses came forward. In 2011, John was asked to come in to the police station to answer some questions. Whenever he was asked about that night or Maria Ridulph he would become aggressive and evasive with his answers. He refused to answer any further questions and was subsequently arrested for the abduction and murder of Maria.

The same month, Maria's tiny body was exhumed and tested for DNA evidence with no luck. A forensic anthropologist examined the skeleton and was able to determine she had been stabbed in the throat with a long blade at least three times. Although this was most likely the cause of death, other causes couldn't be ruled out due to the lack of soft tissue, with which other injuries such as strangulation may have been identified. Nevertheless, the case was pursued and a trial set.

A Long-Awaited Trial

John went to trial in September 2012 for the murder of Maria. Evidence and testimonies were heard from those who had been involved in the case, as well as from some inmates who claimed John had confessed to the murder while awaiting trial. One claimed John said he strangled her with a wire, while another claimed John said he smothered her accidentally while trying to stop her from screaming. On September 14, he was found guilty of the abduction and murder of Maria and was given a life sentence. A parole period of twenty years was given, however, John was seventy-three years of age at the time of the sentencing.

John filed a petition for post-conviction relief in 2015, and after extensive investigation by the state's Attorney, it was determined that he was innocent. A court hearing took place in March 2016 and the conviction was overturned. The dismissal of the charge of murder was without prejudice, which means that another charge of murder of Maria Ridulph could be brought against him in the future.

CHAPTER 11:

CAPTIVE FOR 24 YEARS – THE JOSEPH FRITZL CASE

This case takes place in a town called Amstetten in Austria, when it was discovered a man had kept his daughter captive for twenty-four years in the basement of the family home. She had been abused, raped, and assaulted, and would not be free until she was forty-two years of age and had birthed seven children by her father. For a daughter to be treated so heinously by a man who is supposed to love and protect her is abominable and that the children they created suffered such psychological damage is horrendous. This man and his wife were the epitome of evil.

An Incestuous Situation

Joseph Fritzl and his wife Rosemarie had a large family, comprised of seven children. There were five daughters and two sons. Elisabeth was born in 1966, and her father began to abuse her from the time she was eleven years old. She went on to complete the required education, and at fifteen she undertook study on waitressing. Elisabeth ran away from home in January 1983 and fled to Vienna with a work friend. The police were notified, and she was found and returned to her parents. Reluctantly, she had to go back, but she did finish her course and was offered a job.

When Elisabeth was eighteen, her father told her he needed help carrying a door down into the basement of the home. She agreed to help and even held the door in place while he attached it to the frame. Little did she know that it was this door that would keep her locked inside. Josef then held a towel soaked in ether over her face, and once she was unconscious, he locked her in the basement.

Following her disappearance, her mother filed a missing person report with the authorities. Josef then began forcing Elisabeth to write letters saying she no longer wanted to live with her family and she had moved away with her friend. One letter stated that if they came looking for her she would flee the country. Josef had also told the authorities that he believed she had joined a religious cult. All of this was nonsense, of course, as she was in the basement of the family home the whole time.

Elisabeth was repeatedly raped by Josef during the twenty-four years he held her captive. She gave birth to seven children without any medical treatment whatsoever. One baby died just after he was born, and three of them were sent upstairs to live with Josef and Rosemarie. They told social services that the children had just appeared on the doorstep, and they were left in their care by the authorities with regular checkups. At no time was there any suspicion by social services as to what was really going on.

After the birth of the fourth child, Josef enlarged the captivity area so that Elisabeth had more space for herself and her children. Instead of bringing her food every few days, she now had a refrigerator to store food in, as well as hotplates to heat the meals up. They now had a radio, a television, and a video player to entertain them. Elisabeth spent her time teaching her children basic schooling, such as how to read and write. If Josef felt they needed punishing, he would switch off their light supply or refuse to bring them food for days at a time. Elisabeth was told by Josef that if they tried to escape, they would all be gassed.

A Visit to the Hospital Invokes Suspicion

The eldest daughter of Elisabeth and Josef, Kerstin, was unwell and fell unconscious on April 19, 2008. Josef agreed to seek medical care for Kerstin, and Elisabeth helped him carry her upstairs. It was the first time Elisabeth had been out of the basement for twenty-four years. She was ushered back to the basement, and Kerstin was sent by ambulance to the hospital. Josef arrived later and said he had found a note by Elisabeth. The staff at the hospital found this very strange and alerted law enforcement on April 21. They made a media appeal for Elisabeth to come forward, and at the same time reopened her missing person's case. Again, Josef reiterated his beliefs that she had joined a cult and produced another letter from January 2008 as the most recent one he had received. It was found that the postmark on the letter was not an area known for cults, and the way the letters were written seemed as though they had been dictated.

Elisabeth was desperate to see Kerstin, and Josef finally agreed on April 26. Once at the hospital, the doctor taking care of Kerstin alerted the police that they were there, and they were subsequently detained and taken to the station for questioning. Elisabeth wouldn't say anything until the police promised her that she would never have to see Josef ever again. She then proceeded to tell them in great detail of her ordeal in the basement and all the horrific things Josef had made her do. Following her statement, Josef was immediately arrested under suspicion of serious crimes committed against family members.

The Trial of Josef Fritzl

Josef's trial was perhaps one of the shortest in history, lasting just four days. He had pled guilty to all charges, included rape, incest, coercion, enslavement, false imprisonment, and the negligent homicide of the baby, Michael, who died shortly after birth due to lack of medical care. He was ultimately sentenced to life imprisonment, while Elisabeth, her children, and her mother were all taken into care. Throughout the trial, more was learnt about the background of Josef. He had a long history of violent crime, including rape and attempted rape. He was also known for indecently exposing himself. Although he had once been incarcerated, the conviction was expunged after a period of fifteen years, so when social services became involved, his background check did not reveal his previous crimes.

The Psychological Scars and Fighting Back to Normality

Following their arrival into care, Elisabeth, the children, and her mother were placed in a clinic where they could receive all the medical and psychological treatment they might need. They were shielded from the prying outside world as they grasped the enormity of what they were going through. The three children who had been kept in the basement and even Elisabeth needed therapy to adjust to natural light after being kept in a semi-dark space for so long. It was also difficult to adjust to having space to move around in.

All were plagued with panic attacks and anxiety. One child was unable to walk properly due to having to stoop for so long in the basement. Another tore her hair out and stuffed her clothing into the toilet. The children that had been kept upstairs had issues with resentment and anger. The treatment and therapy for Elisabeth and her children will be an ongoing need for many years to come.

CHAPTER 12:

A CONTROVERSIAL CASE OF POLICE MISCONDUCT – OR WAS IT MURDER BY COP?

Nizah Morris was an entertainer who also happened to be transgender. She had been living as a female since her early 20s, and her day job was working for her mother at her daycare center. At night she would perform in a drag show at a bar called Bob and Barbara's in Philadelphia's Center City. She was also a practicing Buddhist, calm by nature and making a good life for herself. Tragically, all that came to an end on December 22, 2002. The controversy that followed would rock the legal system and create support from all walks of life for the rights of transgender people.

Nizah Morris Left Lying in the Street

Nizah had been to a party at a bar located at the intersection of Chancellor and Juniper streets in Philadelphia. The bar was called the Key West Bar, and she reportedly left at around 2 a.m. On exiting the bar, Nizah collapsed on the ground outside, intoxicated. Those who were outside the bar formed a group around her and alerted the paramedics. Nizah was unable to even stand unsupported at this point.

An officer from the 6th District police precinct arrived, and because Nizah refused to go to hospital the ambulance was cancelled. Instead, the police officer offered her a ride to the hospital, but she declined this also. All Nizah wanted to do was go home. Those who were nearby helped Nizah into the police car, and the officers proceeded to take her home. Her address was in the 5000 block of Walnut Street, but the officers claimed she wanted to be let out of the car at 15th and Walnut streets. They noticed her walking towards 16th Street.

Just minutes later, a motorist driving by saw Nizah lying on the sidewalk. She had an injury on the side of her forehead that was bleeding, and a call was made to 911 asking for medical assistant. This time an officer for the 9th District precinct arrived. A call was not made to a supervisor, and the situation was not considered nor treated as a crime.

By the time Nizah arrived at hospital, her condition was critical. Life support was removed on December 23 and she was pronounced dead on December 24 at 8:30 p.m. The medical examiner ruled the death as a homicide on December 25, but the police department's homicide unit would not accept it. They instead classified it as an accidental death. A second opinion was then requested.

Police Request a Second Opinion

The controversy surrounding this case was whether or not the police officers acted appropriately in their interactions with Nizah that night. For starters, even though she was refusing medical treatment in the first instance, the ambulance should not have been cancelled. Also, even though the police officers were not required to drive her home, once they had agreed to do so, they were responsible for getting her home safe and sound. They certainly shouldn't have dropped her off elsewhere and let her walk off when earlier she couldn't even stand unaided due to her level of intoxication. If it was only minutes later that she was found injured on the sidewalk; the officers couldn't have been watching her walk away safely.

The family, friends, and the community in general had many questions regarding what happened to Nizah that night. It would be easy to assume it was an accident—she was drunk and quite easily could have fallen and whacked her head. But, the medical examiner called it a homicide. So who was the perpetrator? Was there an assailant or was it homicide by negligence and failure to provide due care?

According to Nizah's family members, the photographs they were shown at the medical examiner's office showed marks on her wrists like indentations, as well as what appeared to be defensive wounds on her hands. The local newspaper ran a story on the tragedy on December 31, but they abhorrently referred to Nizah as a prostitute and a male. This further fueled the fires that were already burning among her family and friends. She was cremated on January 1, 2003, with more than 300 people attending the service.

A second opinion was sought from a brain injury specialist. The tests undertaken showed that she had died due to a cerebral injury, otherwise known as a brain injury. On January 30, the homicide division declared the case a homicide.

There were numerous inconsistencies in the police reports from that night in relation to witness statements. Protests were being held due to the handling of the case by the police department.

There were issues surrounding Nizah not being identified for nearly 64 hours while she was in the hospital, despite her fingerprints being on record. One of the officers present actually knew Nizah, but he did not identify her either. Those who had been at the scene also told the police officers who Nizah was, but this information was never passed on either.

There were too many questions and not enough answers, and the community was rallying for further investigation. In April 2003, the District Attorney launched an investigation into the case, but it would be short-lived and provided no answers at all, just more questions.

The Investigation into the Officers

The investigation started by the District Attorney quickly ended in December, failing to find who was responsible for Nizah's death. The DA appealed to the public for help, and declared at the same time that the three police officers involved in the incident had all acted appropriately. Complaints were lodged by Nizah's mother against the police department for not providing all of the information to the family. A civil suit was brought against the bar that allowed Nizah to become intoxicated, as well as the officers involved, the EMTs, and the city of Philadelphia, by the Center for Lesbian and Gay Civil Rights. Interestingly this suit was settled in May 2004 for $250,000.

Police Advisory Commission Called In

An initial investigation undertaken by the Police Advisory Commission asserting that the only officer who hadn't acted properly that night was an Officer Skala. The Philadelphia Police Department advised the Commission within days that they had not received all of the documentation, as some of it was missing, including the homicide report, which had been missing since 2003. As a side note, this report miraculously reappeared in 2011 in the archives.

The Commission voted to reopen the investigation in March 2008. This investigation proved to be fruitless and pointless, so the initial findings remained standing. Once again they voted to reinvestigate in 2011, and at the end of the investigation they called for the U.S. Attorney General's Office to fully investigate the case. They in turn, declined. By 2015, the only result from all of the investigations was that Officer Skala received a verbal reprimand, even though it was found that she had lied and deliberately deceived the department about her interactions with Nizah that night. She eventually ended up working in the commissioner's office—what a punishment! No wonder so many people lost their faith in the Philadelphia legal system.

Something Good from Something Bad

In honor of Nizah, Philadelphia opened a center for drug addiction treatment for transgender persons. The official name is 'The Morris Home for Trans and Gender-Variant People'. To date it is the only inpatient center of its kind that is run by transgender people for transgender people. Nizah may have lost her life, but in her name she is helping others to save theirs.

TRUE CRIME STORIES

12 Shocking True Crime
Murder Cases

True Crime Anthology Vol.3

By
Jack Rosewood

INTRODUCTION

The world is a wonderful place, full of many amazing sights and people that bring joy to people's lives. We see the things that bring joy to people every day in a variety of different ways, from the smile of a child to the relaxing calm of nature. With that said, the world can also be an incredibly cruel and awful place that is full of heartless killers and deranged criminals. Because of the juxtaposition between joy and cruelty that the world presents, it is sometimes difficult for us to navigate around the darkness in order to enjoy the light.

Most people will never witness the cruel side of the world, but unfortunately those who do are often innocent and completely unaware of their situations.

Most of us have read or heard about the statistics that state the perpetrators of violence usually attack someone they know. We would like to think that we can defend against such attacks, or at least see them coming; but when a stranger attacks, it creates an entirely different dynamic for law enforcement and society.

Seemingly random acts of murder and mayhem leave the surviving victims and their families in pain and society wondering what would drive a person to commit such acts. Worse yet are the cases where a hapless victim is taken off the streets and murdered, only for the killer to escape justice.

In the following pages of this book, you will read about several crime cases from around the world where heinous crimes were committed by depraved souls, often at random. Most of these cases were eventually solved through diligent police work and a few lucky breaks.

But one of the most horrendous of these crimes, the Keddie cabin murders, still remains open.

Many of the crimes profiled in the pages of this book concern spree killers, often from countries with low crime rates. Oftentimes these killers used guns to claim their victims, like Christian Doriner, Mattias Flink, and Colin Ferguson; but others, such as Matthew Tvrdon, have proved that you do not need a gun to inflict multiple casualties.

So open the pages of this book, if you dare, and learn about some of the most bizarre crime cases from around the world in recent history.

CHAPTER 1:
THE MELANIEE ROAD MURDER CASE

Most people look back on their seventeenth year of life with fondness. Independence is right around the corner, but the protection of family and the law still allows one a level of comfort not known in adulthood. Many of us pushed and even broke the limits of family rules and the law at seventeen by experimenting with drugs, alcohol, and sex. But the majority of us come through that rebellious period a bit wiser and eventually move on to become productive members of society.

Of course there are those who never leave their adolescent rebellion behind and instead immerse themselves in various criminal activities.

Then there are those who never move past the rebellious attitude of age seventeen because they are murdered by people who continue to indulge their adolescent fantasies, no matter how old they are or how twisted the nature of their fantasies.

Melaniee Road was a seventeen-year-old whose flirtation with rebellion was randomly ended in murder one June night in 1984 by a sadistic killer. Melaniee's murder shocked and outraged her fellow British citizens who asked questions that could not be answered because there were few leads for the police to follow.

Eventually, due to advances in technology, Melaniee's murderer was eventually arrested and sent to prison, but the killer's capture only seemed to raise more questions in a case that was as bizarre as it was heart wrenching.

A Good Girl

In 1984, seventeen-year-old Melaniee Road was not the typical murder victim in the United Kingdom. She was a good student who was set to go to college, enjoyed spending time with her family, friends, and boyfriend, and was not involved in any criminal activity or drug use.

The attractive blonde also had no known enemies.

Because of her background, police were baffled as to who killed the young woman on the quiet streets of Bath on the morning of June 9, 1984.

A Vicious Attack

The night of June 8, 1984, began like many others for Melaniee Road. She met up with her boyfriend early in the evening and then the two walked to one of their favorite hangouts, the "Beau Nash" nightclub, where they met some friends.

After an evening of dancing and drinking, the group decided to call it a night at about 1:30 am, so they all said their goodbyes and went their separate ways. Melaniee had made the walk from her parent's home to the club and back numerous times without incident. In 1984, Bath had a low crime rate and there were no high crime areas she had to pass between the club and her house.

Unfortunately, she met a monster on her walk home.

Although there were no witnesses to the attack, police were able to piece together the sequence of events through physical evidence.

Melaniee's attacker mercilessly pounced on her on the sidewalk, stabbing her multiple times before she ran into a cul-de-sac. The cul-de-sac proved not only to be a dead end for the street, but also for Melaniee as the attacker then stabbed her several more times, twenty-six total. As the young woman lay bleeding to death on the lonely street, the killer could not contain his sadistic urges, so he raped her lifeless body.

Melaniee's body was discovered a few hours later in a pool of blood by a milkman who was making his daily deliveries with his ten-year-old son.

The local police immediately sealed the location and took biological evidence from the body, but DNA profiling was still unavailable to police departments in 1984.

With no biological evidence that they could immediately use, detectives turned to more traditional methods in order to capture Melaniee's killer. Attention was first focused on Melaniee's boyfriend, but it was quickly determined that he was not the killer as he had an air-tight alibi.

The police then received a tip that a young woman and a man were heard arguing loudly in the vicinity around the time of the murder. Investigators followed up the lead, but it proved to be another dead end.

Finally, with most of their resources exhausted and at their wit's end, the local police initiated "Operation Rhodium." The operation was essentially a dragnet in which ninety- four men who fit the profile of the killer were rounded up and arrested on various charges ranging from outstanding warrants to minor offences such as loitering. The operation proved to be a failure and worse yet the killer was one of the men arrested.

The killer had slipped right through their hands!

The Case Goes Cold

Unfortunately, due to scientific limits regarding DNA profiling and a lack of eye witnesses, the Melaniee Road murder case quickly went cold. It was not as if the young woman's family gave up; they continued to press the case in the media and with the local police. In the mid-1980s there was simply nothing the police could do, but the amount of biological evidence the killer left on Melaniee's body meant that eventually time was on the investigators' side.

Today, the process of DNA profiling has become so ubiquitous that few actually stop to consider the science or history behind it. Because we have become inundated with so many true crime documentaries and a plethora of crime procedural dramas, many think that DNA is something that is left behind at every crime scene and can be simply collected by investigators, leading to an arrest, all within a matter of hours.

Of course, the process is not so simple and it took a long time for it to become refined to the point where it is today.

Deoxyribonucleic acid (DNA), the building block of living organisms, was first identified by Swiss scientist Friedrich Miescher in 1869. The first several decades of DNA research focused on identifying and isolating inherited diseases, but the biggest advance, at least in terms of forensic police work, came in a lab in Leicester, United Kingdom. British scientist Alex Jefferys, from his Leicester lab just months after Melaniee's murder, discovered that each person has a unique DNA code that can be "fingerprinted."

Jefferys first used DNA profiling to help capture British murderer and rapist Colin Pitchfork in 1987, which set the stage for DNA profiling to be used in crime labs across the world.

Despite DNA profiling offering new hope to Melanie Road's family, the process had many problems in its first two decades of use. Samples too small or degraded, as was the case with Melanie Road, were often unable to be used and the process itself could take several months to create a complete profile. Databases that stored DNA profiles of criminal offenders also took several years to launch as time was needed for the computer technology to catch up with the advances made in DNA profiling.

By the early 2010s, the United Kingdom had amassed an extensive DNA database of criminal offenders so the authorities thought it was a good time to take another look at the Melanie Road murder case. The police began by taking DNA samples from hundreds of local Bath men, as well as rechecking the database for any hits.

But little did they know that the big break in the case would come from the DNA of a woman, not a man.

A Circuitous DNA Match

Clara Hampton never had the perfect life. She never seemed to end up in a good relationship and in 2014, at the age of forty-four, she found herself in another such situation with her, live-in boyfriend. The two became involved in a heated situation that turned physical, which resulted in the police showing up. Clara was booked on a minor charge that required her to give a mouth swab for the United Kingdom's DNA database.

The swab quickly put things in motion that solved the thirty-year murder mystery of Melanie Road.

Shortly after Clara's DNA was entered into the database, investigators working on the Road case were electrified to learn that they had a *partial* hit. DNA profiling had advanced quite a bit since 1987 so by 2014 scientists were able to match a sample with a *similar* profile. When investigators learned that the similar profile was from a woman, they knew that she did not commit the crime, but instead it was probably someone closely related to her, like a brother.

Or perhaps her father, Christopher John Hampton, who was originally brought in for questioning as a suspect during Operation Rhodium in 1984.

Hampton, who lived on the street where Melanie was murdered in 1984, was quickly picked up by police and given a DNA test. The findings were conclusive.

"Christopher Hampton's DNA was found to match the DNA from semen stains on the fly and crotch of Melaniee Road's trousers," said prosecutor Kate Brunner.

When the sixty-four-year old Hampton appeared in court, it was quickly revealed that he did not fit the typical psychological profile of such a killer. He was the father of four children and had been gainfully employed as a house painter throughout his life. Hampton also did not have a criminal record and was never linked to any criminal activity or drug use.

But it was all apparently just a façade, a mask, for a truly devious mind and soul that always lurked beneath.

The Trial and Unanswered Questions

Facing a mountain of physical and circumstantial evidence, Hampton decided to forgo a trial and instead pled guilty to murder in May 2016. When Hampton appeared in front of a judge for sentencing, he was a shell of his former self. He looked tired of life and gazed with no affect as the judge read the sentence.

Judge Andrew Popplewell looked straight at Hampton, sentenced the killer to a twenty two year minimum prison sentence, and said, "You will very likely die in prison." Because the United Kingdom does not have the death penalty and the crime rate is much lower there than in the United States, true "life sentences" are rarely given; but due to Hampton's age, as the judge said, the sadistic killer will likely die in prison.

After Hampton was sentenced, Melanie Road's friends and family said in interviews that they were glad the ordeal was finally over and that they were now able to find some closure, although the pain will never fully subside. They also indicated that were happy knowing that Hampton will never be able to victimize another young woman.

With that said, there are still some unanswered questions in the Melanie Road murder case.

"It hurts beyond repair," said Jean Road, mother of Melanie. "How can he do that to somebody and then live with people and with them not knowing?"

But somehow Christopher Hampton was able to keep his

diabolical act a secret from those closest to him for over thirty years. Most people would never consider committing such a heinous crime and those who do often confess after several years out of guilt.

Apparently, Christopher Hampton has no conscience because one is required to feel a sense of guilt.

Hampton's lack of empathy and his apparent ability to keep his mouth shut leads one to wonder if he left more victims strewn about the United Kingdom. Presently, his DNA has not been linked to any other cold cases in the UK's database, but as the Melanie Road case proved, sometimes a strange coincidence and several years are needed to crack a cold case.

CHAPTER 2:

THE KEDDIE CABIN MURDERS

Plumas County, California, is located in the northeast part of the state in the Sierra Nevada Mountains. The county is not very large in population, just over 20,000 inhabitants according to the 2010 census, but is quite large in size, which has resulted in a sparsely populated region where people have plenty of room to spread out.

The county was part of the gold rush in the middle of the nineteenth century, but has largely been bypassed in a number of ways in the 150 plus years since. There are no US highways or Interstates that run through the county and jobs have been as scarce as gold in more recent decades. Although the cost of living is quite low by California standards, the lack of employment and its isolation have combined to make Plumas County a place where few people move to who are looking for opportunities or to start over.

But starting over is exactly why Glenna Sue Sharp moved to Plumas County with her five children in 1980, except it turned out to be a fatal move and eventually ended up as one of the most bizarre cases in the annals of criminal history.

The Horror in Cabin 28

On the morning of April 12, 1981, the bodies of thirty-six-year old Glenna Sue Sharp, her fifteen-year-old son John Sharp, and his friend seventeen-year-old Dana Wingate were found beaten and stabbed to death in the living room of the Keddie, California, cabin that the mother shared with her children. The brutality of the crime shocked area residents and later the nation, as the victims appeared to have been killed randomly in a county that was known for having a low crime rate. As different media outlets quickly disseminated the details of the horrific attack, a new, appalling detailed was revealed.

Glenna's twelve-year-old daughter Tina was missing!

The Plumas County Sherriff's Department was quickly overwhelmed with the rapidly evolving situation—they had a triple murder *and* a missing person case on their hands. From the beginning, the investigation was bungled, which led to the Keddie cabin murders becoming a cold case that will probably never be solved.

Unfortunately, the victims of the Keddie cabin murders were in many ways the perfect victims: they were poor, had no powerful connections, and were not from the area.

The Sharp Family

When the perpetrator of a murder is not immediately known to detectives, their investigation usually begins with the victims. The police often begin their search of the victim, or in this case victims, backgrounds for signs of drug use or criminal activity. If neither of those are determined to be contributing factors in a person's murder, then investigators look at the victim's finances and/or if he/she may have been involved in a love triangle. In most cases, detectives are usually able to ascertain quickly that the victim was involved in one of these situations.

But in the case of the Keddie cabin murders, it was soon realized that a motive was not so clear.

A look the background of Glenna Sue Sharp, who usually went by her middle name, revealed that she was a divorced mother who was originally from Connecticut, but moved to northern California in 1980 to start over with her five children: John, Tina, ten-year-old Rick, five-year-old Greg, and fourteen-year-old Sheila. Plumas County investigators quickly ruled out a custody dispute gone bad because Sue's ex-husband was nowhere in the area when the crime happened and did not have the means to hire a killer. Also, the crime did not fit the typical custody dispute murder, as one of the children was killed and another was missing.

Sue did have money problems though.

The single mother found it difficult to find work that paid enough to support her five children, even though they lived in a relatively cheap cabin in an affordable county. Because of this, Sue was forced to rely on government assistance in order to make ends meet, but there was no evidence that she was in debt to loan sharks or any other criminal types.

Sue was described by her neighbors and acquaintances as a loner who spent most of her time with her children and let few people from outside of her familial circle get very close. She was known to date a few men in the area, but was not involved in a serious relationship at the time of her murder and none of her former suitors were known to harbor any acrimony towards her.

Sue was also not involved in any major drug activity and the police believed the other victims were simply too young to have created enemies who would go to such lengths for revenge.

The victims' backgrounds provided the Plumas County Sherriff's Department with few clues.

What is Known about the Crime

Despite finding dead ends with the victims' backgrounds, investigators found a mountain of physical evidence in the Sharp's cabin and were also lucky to have a possible eyewitness to the crime and numerous witnesses to the events that immediately led up to the horrific murders.

According to the accounts of surviving members of the Sharp family, as well as those from the Smartt family who lived next door in cabin 27, John Sharp and Dana Wingate were last seen walking down a road near the cabin on the evening of April 11. The two boys were hanging out that evening and planned to stay in John's basement bedroom, but were found the next morning dead in the upstairs living room.

The fact that the two boys were found dead in the living room with Sue Sharp was indeed mysterious to begin with, but it became even more so when investigators learned that John's bedroom did not have an entrance that led to the cabin. The only door in his downstairs bedroom led to the outside.

As the facts of the case came to light, it soon became obvious that the Keddie cabin murders were as enigmatic as they were brutal.

When Sheila Sharp returned home from a sleepover next door, she never imagined the horror that she would find. Almost immediately, the authorities suspected that more than one assailant was involved.

Murder in the real world is often a much more difficult affair than on television. It takes several minutes to kill someone from strangulation and beating and/or stabbing a person to death is usually quite loud and also takes some time. The killers are also often injured in stabbing and beating deaths. The fact that there were three victims suggests that either multiple assailants subdued the victims in a concerted attack, or a lone assailant used a gun to pacify the victims and then had one of his victims help bind the other two.

The victims were all bound with medical tape and electrical wires. The ligatures used on Sue were actually quite complex and suggest that she may have been the primary target and the other two were "collateral damage." The complex ligatures also suggest that the killer practiced ahead of time, had made ligatures before, or was possibly involved in a trade where knot tying was important.

Both Sue and John were stabbed several times and had their throats slit. Sue was also bludgeoned by what was later determined to be a pellet gun, although it was never recovered.

Some believe that Dana was forced to help the attacker(s) bind the other two and then he was killed last. The method of his murder was slightly different. He was strangled and then beaten with a hammer that was recovered several years later. Sue, John, and Dana suffered truly brutal deaths, which suggests that a personal vendetta was aimed at one of them. Since both of the boys were young and not known to be involved in criminal activity, the police believed that the primary target was Sue, but as will be discussed more below, determining a motive for her murder has been elusive.

A crime of truly horrific proportions took place in the Sharp family cabin on the night of April 11 or the early morning of April 12, which left the local authorities initially both baffled and alarmed, but the search for clues only seemed to turn up more questions instead of answers.

The sleepover that Shelia returned from was in cabin 27, which was located next door only about fifteen feet away. Neither she nor anyone in the cabin heard anything on the night of the eleventh or the morning of the twelfth. One would think that the brutal murders of three people would have created some significant sounds—a victim screaming, thuds of the bodies, or perhaps the killer(s) leaving the scene of the crime.

Even more amazing was the fact that three children were asleep in the room *next* to where the murders took place.

When the Plumas County Sherriff's Department cleared the crime scene, they soon discovered that Greg and Rick Sharp, along with neighbor boy, twelve-year-old Justin Smartt, were in a bedroom that was located on the other side of a wall from where the murders took place. Deputies pulled the three boys from one of the bedroom windows, but they were stunned to learn that none of them heard any commotion during the night. They apparently slept through the entire event!

Once the authorities learned what had happened, they were then faced with another problem—Tina was missing. In the weeks, months, and years following the Keddie cabin murders, the local authorities were criticized for not doing more to find Tina and taking too long to begin the search. Once the search began, efforts were made to find the girl with 1981 technology. Helicopters, dogs, horseback search teams, and distribution of Tina's picture on flyers around the area were all employed to find the girl, but they were all to no avail.

In 1984, in neighboring Butte County about thirty miles from Keddie, remains of an adolescent female skull were discovered in a rural area. The remains were later determined to be those of Tina Sharp—the number of Keddie cabin murder victims went to four.

THE INVESTIGATION

From the beginning, the investigation of the Keddie cabin murders was flawed. It is true that the Plumas County Sherriff's Department did not have, and still does not have, the resources or seasoned investigators that larger police departments possess, but their investigators made a number of major mistakes throughout the investigation pertaining to witness interviews, crime scene investigation, evidence storage, and the search for Tina. Those who have followed the case over the last thirty-five years point to the mistakes of the Plumas County Sherriff's Department as the primary reason why the case has never been solved.

One of the biggest problems in the investigation was the eyewitness account of Justin Smartt. During his interview with investigators, Smartt at first claimed to have seen two white males leave cabin 28 sometime during the night. Sketch artists were brought in and composites were created of the two possible suspects, but Smartt's story began to change. In subsequent interviews, Smartt claimed that he thought what he saw that night was actually part of a dream. The boy's confusion was natural considering the traumatic event he lived through, which could have been remedied with other interrogation methods such as hypnotism.

But investigators apparently lost interest in Smartt and turned their energies elsewhere.

Another mistake that is often pointed to by critics of the police who have investigated the Keddie cabin murders in more recent years is the lack of proper crime scene management by the Plumas County Sherriff's Department. Investigators and even civilians were allowed to walk through the scene, perhaps destroying valuable forensic evidence in the process.

In fairness to the Plumas County Sherriff's Department, 1981 was several years before DNA profiling was a reality and almost fifteen years before the CODIS system was operational in the United States. With that said, police departments in 1981 knew that not only was proper management of a crime scene vital to a criminal investigation, but that the correct collection and storage of biological and forensic evidence was essential to solving a case.

Although DNA profiling was not known yet, blood typing did exist in 1981, and of course fingerprint identification had been used for about 100 years at that point. If the biological and forensic evidence in the Keddie cabin murders had been stored in the Plumas County crime lab properly, they may have led to the perpetrator(s) being caught at a later time.

Unfortunately, all of the forensic evidence connected to the Keddie cabin murders has been either lost or destroyed. When asked about the situation, the Plumas County Sherriff's Department refused to comment to the media on the missing evidence and in fact have been seen as somewhat hostile towards the media on this topic. The Plumas County Sherriff's Department also, for the most part, refused the help of state and federal agencies in the Keddie cabin murders. The overall attitude of the Plumas County Sherriff's Department towards the media and outsiders has been viewed as mysterious and suspicious by many and has raised several questions.

Why would the Plumas County Sherriff's Department, which was understaffed and ill-equipped to handle such a high profile case, not welcome the help of California state and federal law enforcement agencies? Does the Plumas County Sherriff's Department have something to hide, or is it just an agency full of stubborn individuals?

Concerned citizens have pressed for answers to these questions for decades.

A Rogues' Gallery of Suspects

Although the Plumas County Sherriff's Department dropped the ball on numerous occasions during the Keddie cabin murders investigation, their investigators quickly turned up a number of potential suspects and persons of interest.

As already mentioned above, Plumas County is a picturesque part of California with a relatively low crime rate—today and in 1981. Most people know their neighbors and it is still, even after the grisly murders, a place where many people keep their doors unlocked.

But underneath the quaint façade of 1981 Plumas County was a seedy underbelly teaming with a rogues' gallery of characters.

The investigation quickly revealed that Plumas County was home to an ample number of drug dealers, biker gang members, sex-offenders, ex-convicts, and various other local toughs. Truly, Plumas County in 1981 in many ways looked less like a Norman Rockwell painting than it did a setting in a rural crime drama such as *Justified* or *Banshee*.

First, there was Tina's teacher who was said to have an unhealthy interest in the girl. The teacher was a suspect and was later convicted of a sex crime, making him a registered sex offender in the state of California.

Then there was Robert Silveria Junior. Silveria, also known as the "Boxcar Killer," was a train hoping hobo who was associated with the violent hobo gang, Freight Train Riders of America (FTRA). Silveria earned quite a reputation among his fellow FTRA members by killing at least nine people throughout the western United States. Silveria was known to be in Plumas County in 1981 and claimed one of his victims not far from the Keddie cabin murder scene.

A couple of local toughs, Dee Jay Lake and Tony Garedakis, were also considered suspects by law enforcement and still are to some who continue to follow the case.

Sue's former boyfriends were also looked at along with other sex offenders and drug dealers who lived within a stone's throw of cabin 28. Despite the plethora of viable suspects, investigators soon began to focus on a pair who lived right next to the Sharp family.

Martin Ray Smartt was the father of Justin Smartt and the husband of Sue Sharp's friend, Marilyn. The Smartt family lived in cabin 26 with one of Martin's friends, a Chicago native named Bo Boubede. The Smartt and Sharp families were by all appearances good neighbors. The children all got along and played with each other, and the adults were also friendly and would occasionally go out together.

But a number of circumstances quickly made Martin and his friend Bo prime suspects in the Keddie cabin murders.

Some of Justin's recollections of the night of April 11 seemed to implicate his father and when investigators questioned Martin, they were left with even more questions.

According to Martin's statements to the Plumas County Sherriff's Department, he, his wife, and Bo Boubede had stopped by the Sharp home on the night of April 11 to ask Sue to join them for some drinks at a local bar. Sue declined and they left, which ended up being the last time anyone saw Glenna Sue Sharp alive. Martin claimed that the three then went to the bar and later returned home.

The story sounded believable to investigators, but it soon became a problem when Marilyn and Bo's stories diverged from Martin's.

Marilyn corroborated most of her husband's story, but added some very interesting details that helped investigators learn more about Martin's personality and his state of mind on the night of the murders. She claimed that the three did indeed go to the bar that night, but Martin became enraged at the volume and type of music being played at the bar. After having a few drinks, Martin led the three back to his home where he then called the bar and shouted some profanities to the bartender about the music. Marilyn then added that Martin was an abusive man who would turn to violence if he did not get things his way, especially with women.

Although Martin Smartt began to look like a more viable suspect, the Plumas County Sherriff's Department was unable to get a truly damning statement from him, but the Justice Department began to take an interest in the case.

In the United States, the crime of murder, no matter how heinous, is almost always covered under state law. Sometimes the FBI will get involved in murder investigations if the suspected killer has traveled across state lines or is believed to be part of some type of terrorist cell, but most murders are usually investigated by local, county, and/or state police. In the case of the Keddie cabin murders, there was also a kidnapping, which falls under the purview of the FBI.

The Justice Department's investigation of the Keddie cabin murders can be described as uninspired and routine at best. Martin Smartt was brought in to their offices in Sacramento for a polygraph exam, which he passed. The focus of the investigation then shifted from Martin to his friend Bo, but in recent years information has been made public that implicates the former in the murders.

Martin Smartt died in 1990, taking to the grave the answers to the Keddie cabin murders, many believe. In 2000, Smartt's former therapist came forward to the media and claimed that Smartt admitted his role in the murders. According to the therapist, Smartt killed Sue Sharp out of anger because she was apparently trying to convince his wife to leave him due to his physical and mental abuse. The two boys were "collateral damage" and Justin Smartt did in fact see his dad leave the cabin that night.

The "confession" sure sounds like solid evidence, but the reality is that even if Smartt were still alive, there is a good chance that it may not be admissible in court, as it was a violation of the doctor-patient privileged relationship. The credibility of the therapist would also be questioned: why come forward at that time and not earlier?

As investigators focused most of their attention on Martin Smartt as their primary suspect, his friend John "Bo" Boubede looked like he may be good as the second man seen outside cabin 28 on the night of April 11, 1981.

As stated above, Bo Boubede was with Martin and Marilyn Smartt on the night of the murders, drinking heavily at the local bar and the Smartt home. When questioned by investigators, Boubede gave numerous conflicting and strange stories that only helped to cast more suspicion on him. For instance, he gave different times concerning when he and the Smartts were at the bar in order to fit an alibi and for some reason he told police that he was impotent. Boubede would have had no reason to tell the police about his erectile dysfunction unless he was attempting to alibi himself for the rape or attempted rape of Sue.

Boubede also told investigators that he was a former police officer.

Even with limited 1981 technology, it did not take investigators long to learn that Boubede was the furthest thing from a cop. He had a record of violence and was a known associate of notorious Chicago hitman Jim Rini.

Boubede, like Smartt, was called into Sacramento to take a polygraph exam and also like his friend he passed. Later, sources revealed that both exams were extremely easy and full of leading questions.

If Boubede was involved in the Keddie cabin murders, he escaped justice in this world when he died in 1988.

Perhaps one of the most interesting and bizarre twists to the Keddie cabin case came a few months after Tina Sharp's skull was discovered. An anonymous call came into the Butte County Sherriff's Department that claimed the recently discovered human skull was that of Tina Sharp. Because DNA profiling did not exist yet in 1984, the phone call proved to be the key to identifying the skull and therefore determining what happened to the missing girl. The call was taped and a backup was made. The police believed that the call would be the break they needed to solve the case.

But for some reason, a law enforcement officer, whose identity remains unknown to the present day, lost both the original and backup tape.

It seems as though someone, or something, wants the Keddie cabin murders to remain a mystery.

The Keddie Cabin Murders Today

As the years went by, the residents of Keddie and Plumas County eventually went back to life as normal. The memories of the horrendous crimes began to recede in the minds of most people and the police investigation seemed to permanently stall. In the era before the Internet, the case still became an urban legend and cabins 27 and 28 became a sort of pilgrimage site for amateur ghost hunters, gawkers, and kids out for some cheap thrills.

Cabins 27 and 28 were demolished in 2004, erasing forever any physical reminders of the horrors that took place there in 1981.

But not everyone has forgotten about the Keddie cabin murders.

A new generation of tech savvy individuals became intrigued with the case, for reasons beyond simple curiosity or macabre fascination like the gawkers mentioned above. The recent generation of interest in the Keddie Cabin murders has seen some talented filmmakers and investigators who have taken it upon themselves to get to the bottom of this bizarre mystery.

Documentarian Josh Hancock wrote a book and produced an accompanying film in 2008 titled, *Cabin 28: The Keddie Murders*. Hancock explores several of the mysterious issues of the case described above in this book and offers his own take on who he believes committed the murders.

There is also a website—keddie28.com—that serves as the clearing house of the ongoing investigation and allows those interested to give their own opinions on the message board.

The Keddie cabin murders may unfortunately never be solved, but if they are it will be because ordinary, everyday citizens with an interest in the case, like Josh Hancock, will uncover definitive proof that reveals the killer or killers.

CHAPTER 3:

JOSEPH "THE AXE MAN" NTSHONGWANA

Most of you reading this are familiar with the case of the "Blade Runner" Oscar Pistorius. For those of you who are not familiar with the case, Pistorius is a South African runner who competed in the 2012 summer Olympics despite being a double amputee. He ran on artificial limbs, which is how he acquired the moniker the Blade Runner because the carbon-fiber prosthetics he uses to run are curved like blades. Pistorius captured the imagination and hearts of people across the world who saw him as a role model for people with disabilities.

But all of that changed when he shot his model girlfriend to death in 2013. In an instant, Pistorius went from national hero to absolute zero.

Pistorius is currently serving a six year prison sentence in a South African prison for the killing and there is no doubt that the charmed life he once knew as a sports star and national hero is now over.

But before the precipitous rise and fall of the Blade Runner, South Africans witnessed another one of their most popular sports stars take a violent fall from his pedestal.

The Axe Man

In 2011, South Africans were surprised to learn that former rugby union star Phindile Joseph Ntshongwana had been charged with the murders of four men. As residents read the details of the crime, their shock turned to horror when they discovered that Ntshongwana hacked to death and decapitated his victims with an axe.

What could make a man who had it all do such a thing?

From Rags to Riches

Ntshongwana was born in the mid-1970s during the height of the Apartheid regime in South Africa. He grew up in a poor segregated neighborhood where one of his primary outlets was sports, but even that was influenced by the social standards of the time. Blacks preferred to play soccer while whites gravitated towards rugby and cricket, but because of his stocky build, Ntshongwana chose rugby as his favorite sport.

Ntshongwana played rugby in segregated leagues for most of his childhood, which only offered advancement to a minimal level for the gifted player. Things changed, though, for Ntshongwana and South Africa when apartheid ended in 1994, giving the young man the chance to play in South Africa's top leagues, thereby earning the type of money and fame that few blacks, or even whites for that matter, could ever dream of.

By the late 1990s Ntshongwana was on his way!

The height of Ntshongwana's career came in 2010 when his team the Blue Bulls won the title of South Africa's top rugby league. The notoriety thrust the thirty-five-year-old

Ntshongwana to the heights of fame and fortune and made him one of the most recognizable and popular figures in South Africa, with both blacks and whites.

But just a year later the life that took decades for Ntshongwana to build came crashing down in a matter of days.

Stalking His Victims

According to Ntshongwana, his charmed life was shattered in March 2011 when he learned that his daughter had been gang-raped and infected with HIV. The rugby player believed that the corrupt and incompetent police in South Africa would not be able to find the rapists, even if they bothered to look, so he decided to take the law into his own hands.

Ntshongwana grabbed a Bible and an axe and drove from his affluent neighborhood to the poverty and crime-stricken townships of Durban in order to find his prey. Witnesses to the crimes and Ntshongwana himself related to authorities the sequence of events, which were as brutal as they were bizarre.

On March 20, 2011, Ntshongwana read scriptures from the Bible and slinked around the township looking for his victims. He took the life of one of his victims that day, the second on the following, the third on day three, and the fourth victim a week later. The fact that a high-profile professional athlete went on a two week killing spree while reading the Bible is bizarre enough—the number of victims and one week "cooling off" period actually places him in the serial killer category—but the details of what he did to his victims truly place this case in the realm of the outlandish.

Court testimonies state that before killing some of his victims,

Ntshongwana stripped naked, rubbed yogurt over his body, and then made his victims lick it off. One can only guess why he did this: probably to emasculate and degrade his victims before killing them, but it is impossible to say for sure. After hacking his victims to death, he then decapitated the bodies, placing the various body parts in garbage cans throughout Durban. Many of his victims' body parts were never found, but a head was discovered in a garbage can one mile from one of Ntshongwana's murder scenes.

When the details of Ntshongwana's crimes were made public, many were horrified, yet others took a more neutral attitude towards the case. Since the end of apartheid, crime has skyrocketed in the African nation, with carjackings, home invasions, and gang-rapes becoming fairly common crimes. In fact, many HIV-infected men from the most backward regions of the country believe that raping a virgin will cure them of the incurable disease. Because of these stark realities, many South Africans have grown numb to even the most brutal reports of crime in their country.

But Joseph Ntshongwana was different; he was after all a wealthy celebrity.

Those who did follow the case soon began to make comparisons with the O.J. Simpson trial in the United States. To some, it was the case of an entitled athlete who thought he was above the law, while to others it was situation where a man was wrongly accused, or perhaps overcharged.

Both sides were able to follow the heavily publicized trial when it took place in the years following the murders.

A Bizarre Trial and New Revelations

After Ntshongwana was arrested, Durban police investigated the accusation that he killed the men in retaliation for raping his daughter. The police announced that they could find no evidence that the former rugby player's daughter was raped.

It seems that Ntshongwana made up a story that would be believable in a country where such crimes are fairly common.

But if the men did not rape his daughter, why did he kill them?

The answer to this question, which is perhaps the first that anyone who knows about the case asks, will probably never be answered if the strange behavior that Ntshongwana exhibited during his trial is any indication of his state of mind.

When Ntshongwana was brought before a judge during his arraignment, he clutched a Bible and spoke in gibberish, or what some have described as "tongues." He interrupted the judge on numerous occasions and shoved the bailiffs when they tried to intercede. To all in observance, Ntshongwana truly looked like a deranged man.

Not long after the fiasco of his arraignment, Ntshongwana's father claimed he suffered from bi-polar disorder.

The groundwork was laid for an insanity defense.

Despite his bizarre behavior in and out of the court room, a judge ruled that Ntshongwana was competent to stand trial in February 2012. Paul Ntshongwana was convicted of five counts of murder in 2014 and sentenced to life in prison without parole.

After the conviction, the South African media quit featuring stories about the crimes of Joseph Ntshongwana so many entirely forgot about the sport star's fall from grace. Although Ntshongwana may have dropped from the thoughts of most people, South African police have kept an open file on the former rugby star. Since his incarceration, Ntshongwana has been accused of kidnaping and raping a woman in a 2010 incident.

Will more notorious crimes be linked in the future to South Africa's Axe Man? Only time and possibly forensic evidence will be able answer that question.

CHAPTER 4:

THE DISAPPEARANCE AND MURDER OF RYAN LANE

The modern world has provided all of us with some pretty amazing things that have made our lives easier. Cars and airplanes have made travel a breeze, while dishwashers, washers, and dryers have allowed us to have easier domestic lives.

And who can live without a smart-phone?

It is true that science and technology have made life in industrialized countries easier in some ways, but psychologists, psychiatrists, and sociologists have argued that our use of, and some would say dependence on, technology in our daily lives has been a major factor in the decline of interpersonal relationships.

One does not have to look very far to see some signs of this trend. Couples at restaurants out for dinner spend more time on their phones then they do talking with each other and people everywhere live in a virtual world where updating their social media sites is more important than developing relationships in the real world.

Marriage has long been considered one of the casualties of the modern age and now that we are firmly in the age of Internet, divorce rates are steadily increasing in the most industrialized nations.

Despite the now ubiquitous nature of divorce in the modern world, most people who find themselves in one eventually move on with their lives. Of course, things are more difficult when children are involved. Custody disputes can quickly turn an amicable divorce into one full of acrimony. Allegations of misconduct can be made and sometimes more than just feelings are hurt. Even so, most custody disputes end peaceably as both parents realize that years of bickering will only serve to further alienate their children and that a child needs to have a good relationship with both parents.

But in some rare cases, one of the parents involved in a custody dispute believes that he or she and the children involved will be better served if the other parent is taken out of the equation.

The Disappearance

In February 2012, Ryan Lane was a twenty-four-year old father living in Calgary, Alberta, who was hoping to get closer to his young daughter. Life had not been particularly easy for Lane. He had trouble finding decent-paying employment and did not get along very well with the mother of his daughter, an ex-girlfriend who had fulltime custody of their child.

Despite these setbacks, Lane was young and determined to put his life on a positive path. He was working and had recently spoken with a lawyer about establishing specific times to see his daughter. His daughter's mother, Sheena Cuthill, was protective of the child to the point of obsession and would rarely let Lane visit her. Initially, Lane was fine with the arrangement, but once he matured a little he decided he wanted to develop a relationship with his child.

Lane won a judgement in family court that allowed him visitation of his daughter. On February 6, 2012, he met with Cuthill at a local pizza restaurant to discuss the details of the visitation agreement.

All seemed well for Lane.

Then the next day Lane received a mysterious call from a stranger who asked to meet with him to discuss a custody arrangement. Lane's family was immediately disturbed by the call and Ryan's father Bruce warned against him going to the meeting.

"What's he gonna do, stab me, or something?" said Ryan to Bruce.

Bruce pleaded with his son to let him come along, but Ryan insisted he go alone, as that was what the caller had stated. Ryan then walked to a nearby strip mall to meet the mysterious caller, but his father followed behind in his car despite his son's objections.

Bruce Lane then watched as his son got into a red pickup, which then drove off.

Ryan Lane was never seen again!

As hours turned to days, it was clear to Ryan Lane's family that something bad had happened to him. A missing person report was filed with the Calgary Police Department, and detectives followed up on the information about the custody dispute, the mysterious caller and the red truck. Although the situation looked suspicious to investigators and the Lane family was sure something had happened to Ryan, the Calgary police had no solid evidence that foul play was involved.

As the cold Calgary winter turned to spring and then summer, news reports of Ryan's disappearance faded and it seemed to some that police interest in the case had also waned.

But the reality was that detectives were looking closely at Sheena Cuthill and her associates due to some tips they had received and a growing amount of physical and circumstantial evidence they had collected.

But there was still no body.

Murderers are sometimes convicted without the body of the victim ever being discovered, but prosecutors will tell you that their job is much easier if they have a body. Juries often tend to be skeptical and require plenty of evidence to convict a person of murder, especially in today's world where both documentary and fictional television shows that profile the use of forensic evidence to solve crimes are commonplace.

In November 2012, the search for Ryan Lane finally came to an end when the charred remains of a human were discovered in a burn barrel in a remote area of northeast Calgary known as Beiseker. Although investigators believed they had found Ryan's final resting place, the degraded nature of the body could not be identified through DNA profiling. A forensic anthropologist was able to determine that the remains were of a person between the ages of nineteen and thirty, which fit Lane's age; but most importantly, a ring that Ryan's family identified as belonging to him was found in the pile of ashes.

It seems the killer or killers had made their first mistake.

The location of Ryan's remains would later prove to be a key piece of circumstantial evidence.

A Plan Gone Awry?

Once Ryan's remains were discovered, homicide investigators were able to piece together the other evidence they had been collecting in the prior months to produce an arrest warrant for Sheen Cuthill, her husband Timothy Rempel, and his brother Wilhelm "Will" Rempel for the murder of Ryan Lane. Based on statements the defendants gave to police and Cuthill's testimony at her murder trial, it was learned that the three plotted against Lane in order to prevent him from seeing his daughter.

According to Cuthill, the initial plan was just to intimidate and scare Lane away, but things quickly got out of hand. She claimed that the three met on the morning of February 6, 2012, at Cuthill's grandmother's home in northeast Calgary to discuss the details of the plan.

"I was expecting there was going to be a little rough-housing. I assumed there was going to be some fighting," stated Cuthill in a Calgary courtroom. "I didn't think what they were going to do to make it succeed."

Cuthill's courtroom testimony was valuable in answering who Ryan Lane met on February 7—Tim and Will Rempel—but it was short on important details. Essentially, Cuthill attempted to shift culpability in the murder from herself to the Rempel brothers.

But the mountain of evidence against all three clearly demonstrated that each was equally responsible for Ryan's death.

The Evidence

When Sheena Cuthill and the Rempel brothers went to trial, they faced an uphill battle trying to refute what seemed like an endless line of evidence against them. Although much of the evidence was circumstantial, there was just so much of it that it could not possibly be explained away and the few bits of forensic evidence the prosecutors did have only served to corroborate the circumstantial evidence.

One of the most damning pieces of physical evidence in the case was the discovery of Ryan Lane's DNA in both Will Rempel's truck, which happened to be red like the one Ryan was seen getting into, and Tim Rempel's jeep. The presence of the DNA could be explained away by a good defense lawyer perhaps, but it did not look good for the two brothers when it was revealed that they were caught on camera cleaning both vehicles inside and out the day of Ryan's disappearance. It was also extremely suspicious that Will sold his truck, which was in good condition, to a salvage yard the next day for the far under blue book value price of just $128.40!

The location where Ryan's remains were discovered also happened to become strong circumstantial evidence used against the Rempel brothers.

The burn barrel was located not far from a neighborhood where the brothers had both lived. Even more incriminating was the fact that both men had also worked at one time at the barrel's exact location!

Perhaps the evidence that contributed most to the legal demise of the three defendants were the details of the crime they sent each other via text messages. Maybe they thought they would never be suspects in any crime if Ryan's body was never found, or possibly they did not think their messages were saved, but the text messages were most damning because they essentially outlined the anatomy and chronology of the murder.

A 2011 series of texts between Cuthill and her husband, just after the courts awarded visitation rights to Lane, clearly implicate the mother in the conspiracy.

"Can I trust Will to have this done without the cops showing up on my doorstep?" Cuthill asked Tim Rempel.

In another message, Cuthill tried to allay Tim Rempel's fears of getting caught.

"You won't have any part in his mister ur gonna behanve n let ur brother deal with it," she texted like a teenager. "I mean it Tim my answer will be no right now I won't even consider it if you have any part of it."

Within a couple of months Tim Rempel's trepidation passed as a text he sent to his wife just two days before Ryan's abduction demonstrates.

"Getting things ready scoured the best spot at the pit."

To add to the incriminating text messages, the police secretly recorded phone conversations between the two brothers. Tim and Will apparently suspected that the police may be on to them because they spoke in a code during their recorded conversations. Many amateur criminals believe that using code words during a phone conversation will impede a police investigation and make prosecution difficult or impossible, but even professional criminals have been sunk by carefully coded phone conversations. One of the major pieces of evidence used against mafia kingpin John Gotti during his trial was a series of phone calls where the dialogue was spoken in code. Experts were able to quickly crack the code, which helped send Gotti to prison for the rest of his life.

But Tim and Will Rempel were no John Gottis!

The code the two brothers used was easily cracked by the Calgary police. One particularly damning conversation clearly had to do with the site where Ryan Lane's body was burned.

"They found the kitchen," Will told Tim after the police discovered Ryan's charred remains. "But as hot as it was, there was no DNA."

The mountain of evidence led the jury to quickly convict all three defendants of first degree murder on April 20, 2016. Even Sheena Cuthill, who testified against her cohorts, could not escape the fate she created for herself. The three killers were given life sentences and will not be eligible for parole for twenty-five years.

CHAPTER 5:

THE TORTURE AND MURDER OF JUNKO FURUTA

Modern Japan is a country that is as peaceful as it is beautiful. The large cities are neat, orderly, and clean and the rural areas are dotted with Buddhist and Shinto temples that add a sense of charm and spirituality to the country. Japan is also known for its extremely low crime rate. Gun crime is nearly unheard of and the types of violent crimes that plague cities in most industrialized countries are rare.

Because of the overall nature of contemporary Japanese society, the next crime profiled in this book shocked not only Japan, but the entire world.

In November 1988, sixteen-year-old high school student Junko Furuta was kidnapped from a Tokyo street in broad daylight and then subjected to weeks of torture before she was murdered. Once the perpetrators were caught, the extent of just how horrific and barbaric the crime was came to light.

In particular, the case was notable for the degree of cruelty the killers showed toward their victim. It was truly a case of "man's inhumanity to man" as the murderers relished the pain they inflicted on Junko. And adding to the sheer level of barbarity of the crime itself was the fact that all of the killers were juveniles.

How could children act in such a depraved manner?

Junko's murder made many in Japan realize that their peaceful nation could not totally escape problems experienced by the rest of the world. The case became a media sensation in the Asian nation and brought to the forefront of public discourse issues such as juvenile crime and how society should deal with the worst offenders.

The Abduction

On November 25, 1988, Junko Furuta was a cute, bright, sixteen-year-old student at Yashio-Minami High School in the Tokyo suburb of Misato. Junko was a good student who looked forward to moving on to college and life afterwards. In fact, Junko had just turned sixteen when her life was tragically changed.

After school let out and Junko said goodbye to her friends, she walked down the street to go home, but a van pulled up next to her, opened its side panel door, and two boys snatched her off the street in broad daylight.

The boys did not kill Junko then and there; that would have been merciful. Instead, Junko's journey through hell had just begun.

Three of the boys who abducted Junko began to pummel her with their fists and feet as the fourth one drove the van through the crowded streets of Tokyo to their hideout in the Ayase district of Tokyo. But this was no ordinary hideout; it was the home that one of the abductors, a man now known as Jo Kamisaku, lived in with his parents.

Once the abductors arrived at Kamisaku's home, they quickly

hurried their victim to the basement, away from the parents. The boys then covered their tracks by making Junko call her parents, telling them that she was staying at a friend's house for a few days.

It would be the last time Junko spoke with her parents.

Being outnumbered and perhaps believing the boys that she would only be gone for a few days, Junko complied with her abductors.

But the days quickly turned to weeks.

The sadistic boys raped and tortured their helpless victim for a total of forty-four days. At first the boys tried to hide their deed from Kamisaku's parents, but they were unable to do so as Junko screamed with pain during their torture sessions. According to courtroom testimony, Junko even made contact with the parents and pleaded with them for her life, but it was to no avail.

The parents later claimed in court that they were afraid of their son because he repeatedly acted violently towards them and was believed to have connections to the Yakuza. The cowardly nature of the parents was one of many unbelievable aspects of this case. The parents could have called the police at any time during the forty-four days to end Junko's plight.

And Junko's plight was truly unimaginable.

The boys took turns beating Junko with an iron bar and when they tired of that they poured lighter fluid on her and lit it. They would then take turns raping her and when they tired of that they shoved fireworks and light bulbs into her orifices. Junko repeatedly passed out from the pain of her torture sessions, so in order to revive their victim the boys would burn her with cigarettes.

Truly, there was no limit to the depravity the boys inflicted on poor Junko.

Junko was deprived of proper food and water during her captivity and was instead forced to eat cockroaches and other bugs the sadists found crawling around the basement. For water they forced her to drink her own urine.

Towards the end of the ordeal, Junko was begging to be killed quickly, but unfortunately the sadistic teenagers were not done having their fun. They tied a cord around her neck, hung her from a pipe, and then used her for a punching bag.

Despite the immense physical and psychological torture that Junko endured during her captivity, she attempted to escape on more than one occasion and even made it to a phone in the upstairs.

But one of the boys captured and subjected her to another round of torture.

On January 4, 1989 Junko Furuta finally succumbed to her injuries and died of shock.

Medical experts were actually amazed that she lived as long as she did, having been deprived of proper food and water and suffering massive internal injuries from repeated beatings. After Junko was dead, none of the boys expressed any remorse for what they had done. Instead, their energies turned from torture to figuring out how to cover up their heinous crime.

When the sadistic juveniles learned that their quarry was dead, they put their limited brains together to come up with a disposal method. The solution they conjured up demonstrated their lack of intelligence and maturity, which ultimately led to their swift capture.

The gang placed Junko's body in an oil drum and then poured in wet concrete. They then left the drum in a vacant factory near the waterfront. It did not take the police very long to find the drum after a concerned witness called in a tip. After Junko was taken out of the concrete filled drum, the case became a headliner grabber throughout Japan and became known as the "concrete-encased high school girl murder case."

An Adult Crime but Juvenile Time

The four killers were quickly arrested, not due to forensic evidence or one of the boys developing a guilty conscience, but because there were actually other boys who witnessed part of Junko's ordeal. Early in the kidnapping, there were a few other boys who were present in Kamisaku's home and knew about what was happening to Junko Furuta. Although these other boys claimed to police that they did nothing to the innocent sixteen-year-old, they, like Kamisaku's parents, also did nothing to help her.

The case immediately grabbed headlines in Japan and throughout the world for a number of reasons. The extreme brutality exhibited by the killers and the lack of empathy they showed their victim is shocking in any country, by any standards, but when those details were juxtaposed with the generally peaceful and polite nature of Japanese society it became difficult for many to reconcile. The fact that the victim was a sweet, innocent girl and the nature of her abduction—in broad daylight near her school—was enough to inspire fear in the hearts of many Japanese parents.

But once the disturbing details of the case were made public, most people's concerns turned to the Japanese justice system and how it was so unprepared to deal with such a situation.

The four juvenile sadists were tried as adults, but had their identities sealed. Since the crime rate in Japan is very low, there is no death penalty and even the worst of all murderers usually are released from prison after only serving a few years.

The four boys decided not to try their luck with a trial and instead pled guilty to the murder and hoped to receive lenient sentences. The boys were given sentences that ranged from just a couple of years to about ten years.

The public and Junko's family were outraged at the short length of the sentences.

And for some reason three of the four boys also believed that the Japanese legal system did not treat them fairly so they appealed to have their sentences reduced!

When the appeals of three of Junko's killers made their way to the desk of Judge Ryuji Yanse, he apparently felt the same as many did throughout Japan. Instead of reducing their sentences, Yanse resentenced the leader to twenty-one years in prison and the other two to five to nine and five to seven year sentences.

Jo Kamisaku never appealed his sentence and served eight years total, mainly in a juvenile facility, but the last year of his sentence was spent in an adult prison. All men involved in the horrific murder of Junko Furuta have since been released. Little is known about how the men spent their time in prison, but they were most likely not victimized behind bars. In an American prison system and in probably most other countries around the world for that matter, such inmates would be ostracized by others and left to be victimized by the inmate gangs and stronger, more street-smart convicts. Japanese prisons are quite the opposite. The guards maintain strict control at all times and the inmates are forced to keep silent and meditate most of the day.

With all their time to meditate, one wonders if any of the four felt even a tinge of remorse for Junko.

Jo Kamisaku did not.

After Kamisaku was released in 1999, he took the surname of one of his supporters. He even found middle-class employment at a tech firm and to those who knew him and his past it seemed as though he was truly reformed.

But leave someone to his own devices long enough and he will show you his true character.

In 2004, Kamisaku got into a heated disagreement with an acquaintance over a woman. As the two men exchanged words, Kamisaku threatened the man's life and bragged how he had killed before—he was one of the killers of the girl encased in the concrete. The man was stunned by the allegation, but refused to relent, so Kamisaku attacked him.

The attack left the man in the hospital and Kamisaku with a seven year prison sentence.

The Aftermath

The kidnapping and murder of Junko Furuta left an indelible mark, a deep scar, on the psyche of the Japanese people. The case was tried in the media just as much as in the courtroom, which made it the biggest criminal case in modern Japanese history. It brought ideas of crime and punishment, particularly in regards to juveniles, to the forefront of the public discourse, which until that time had been given little attention and was considered a taboo public topic by many.

The Japanese media also found ways to exploit Junko's murder for profit.

Many books were written and films were produced about the case. A couple of the books were more academic in nature and explored the reasons why young men would commit such a crime, but most of the written material published was of a more popular and sensationalistic nature.

It seems the Japanese learned from the Americans how to profit from crime!

One of the better known films produced about the Junko Furuta murder is titled in English, *The Concrete-Encased High School Murder Case*. The movie is a 1995 exploitation film directed by Katsya Matsumura, who is a legend in the genre of Japanese exploitation films. It is a graphic interpretation of the crime that some think glorifies the sadists to a certain degree.

As books and films were being made about Junko's terrible ordeal, her family was quietly forgotten by most in Japan, which does not mean they did not try to make their voices heard. They voiced their anger to the press over what they and many considered light sentences for their daughter's killers and later won a civil lawsuit against Kamisaku's parents.

But no matter how much money they were awarded, it will never erase the forty-four days of hell that Junko endured at the hands of four sadistic teens.

CHAPTER 6:
CHRISTIAN DORNIER'S RURAL FRENCH MASSACRE

The recent terrorist attack at Bastille Day festivities in Nice, France, shocked the world and demonstrated how vulnerable public gatherings can be. For many, it forever darkened with blood a day that is usually reserved for revelry, making it impossible for many to enjoy future celebrations on July 14.

But many French citizens who are old enough will tell you that the Nice attack was not the first time Bastille Day celebrations were interrupted because of violence.

Before the 2016 Bastille Day terrorist attacks, France endured a massacre just two days before the national holiday in 1989; but the perpetrator was not a foreign born terrorist with extremist views. He was an average Frenchman who snapped and killed fourteen people.

The shooter was a thirty-one-year old farmer named Christian Dornier who woke up on the morning of July 12, 1989 with one purpose—to paint the streets of the tiny village of Luxiol with the blood of its citizens!

By the time Dornier's murder spree was over, fourteen people were dead and eight more were wounded from gunshots. Dornier's massacre shook the sense of security of the people in a region that was quite familiar with guns, but not gun violence.

Luxiol, which is located about 270 miles northeast of Paris near the Swiss border, could be the picture on a postcard with its bucolic, idyllic setting. Nestled between fields and farms, the village only has about 140 inhabitants and at least as many guns.

Although few countries afford their citizens a constitutional right to bear arms as the United States does, a quick examination reveals that gun laws run on a continuum around the world. Even in Europe, gun laws are not uniform and go from the extremely restrictive, such as in the United Kingdom, to fairly lax and not unlike American laws as can be witnessed in Switzerland.

France has traditionally fit somewhere in the middle of the continuum. Since it is a country with large rural areas and a substantial population of farmers—it is one of the only nation-states in the world with the ability to feed its own population— France has traditionally allowed its rural inhabitants to keep shotguns and some rifles. Handguns and some high powered rifles are more difficult to obtain, but the government has generally taken a lax attitude towards its farmers possessing firearms.

But the Christian Dornier case was just as much about France's mental health industry as it was about the nation's rural gun culture because Dornier showed all the signs of being mentally unhinged before the killing spree.

Christian Dornier

Christian Dornier was born on July 12, 1958, to farmer Georges Dornier and his wife Jeanne. Christian and his younger brother and sister spent most of their time around the family farm when they were not in school. Like most farm kids, Christian and his siblings helped with chores around the farm before and after school, so their lives were busy. With that said, although a lot was expected from the Dornier children, the parents always provided for their children and there were no reports of abuse in the home.

After graduating from high school, Christian did a brief stint in the French army as a conscript. He was discharged honorably from the military, but family and friends said that when Christian returned home he was not the same.

Although as a boy Christian was always a bit shy, after his military service he turned into even more of a recluse and became a true loner. He preferred being alone to the company of others and spent most of his free time either reading or hiking in the local forests.

He had no friends and never dated.

"He had no friends, hardly ever talked to anybody," said his brother Serge just after the massacre. "We knew he was going to create havoc one day and the police should have dealt with him."

As they say though, "hindsight is 20/20", so it is difficult to place blame in such a matter afterwards.

Or is it?

As Christian spent his days in the forests or between the covers of a book, his father was getting older and began to think about the future of the family farm. Instead of selling the farm to a neighbor, Georges decided that he would follow tradition and cede the farm over to his oldest son upon his death, which would be contingent upon Christian learning the trade.

At first Christian seemed to be willing to prove himself to his father. He began taking farming classes at the local vocational college, but quit after a couple of weeks and then became even more withdrawn than before. Seeing that his oldest son was not up to the responsibility of running the family farm, Georges took Christian's name out of the will.

When Christian learned that he would not inherit the family farm, he sulked rather than confront his father on the matter. Throughout his life, Christian was decidedly a passive-aggressive type personality. He rarely argued with individuals, but he was also known to explode with anger in certain situations.

The first months of 1989 witnessed a dramatic and violent turn in Christian's personality.

He was picked up by the police for an incident in which he threw some rocks at a local woman. In the small town where everyone knew each other, including the police, Christian's parents were simply alerted to the incident.

But the rock throwing was not a simple incident.

Christian then brought his violence to the next level.

The recluse took the Dornier family's shotgun and fired a shot at Georges and another one at their neighbor. It is not known if Christian was trying to hit either of the men and missed, or if he was trying to scare them, or if it was to get attention. He succeeded on both counts, as the two frightened men called the local police on the disturbed Christian once more. Unlike the rock throwing incident where Christian was picked up and released to his family, the courts became involved. Although Christian was allowed to return to his family's home, he was ordered to see a psychiatrist.

At first, the visits to the psychiatrist seemed to have helped Christian, but he carried a rage that could not be quenched by a few visits to a shrink.

When Christian's sister Corrine was married on July 8, he was the only immediate family member not in attendance. Instead, Christian spent the day driving back and forth through the village in his Volkswagen Golf. Perhaps he was trying to exorcise his demons or maybe he was going through a dry run of his massacre.

The Massacre

July 12, 1989 began like a normal day for the residents of Luxiol. Some people got up early to take care of their chores, while others began their preparations for Bastille Day, which was only two days away. The residents were happy and content.

They did not know what was in store for them.

For most people a birthday is a day to celebrate with family and close friends, but for Christian Dornier, July 12, his birthday, would be the day when he went to war against the world.

Christian slept late on his birthday and refused to have lunch with his family. Just after lunch the French spree killer would begin his reign of carnage, but he first needed a weapon. After he and the neighbor were shot at by Christian, Georges made sure to hide all of the family's guns in secure locations—except for one.

When Christian learned that his father was hiding all of the family's firearms, he managed to hide one himself in the kitchen.

Christian Dornier would need only one gun.

Just before 2:30 pm Christian moved his brother-in-law's car so that he could later move his VW out of the driveway. He then calmly went back into the kitchen and waited.

At 2:30 he heard a car door slam in the driveway, which he believed was his brother Serge. As soon as the front door of the house began to open, Dornier let loose with the first homicidal shot from his shotgun. His victim fell to the ground instantly, dead.

It was not his brother Serge whom Christian had just killed, but a cattle inseminator named Marcel Lechine. Despite not hitting his intended target, Dornier did not hesitate and turned the gun and shot and killed his sister at point blank range. He then shot his sixty-three-year-old father in the neck, wounding him.

In the confusion of the initial shooting spate in the kitchen, Georges was able to run from the house to a neighbor's for help. Georges yelled for help as he ran to the neighbor's door, confused and bleeding.

Georges' cries for help went unheeded though as his son recovered his bearings, chased him down, and killed him with a single shot to the back.

After dispatching his father, Christian then returned to the Dornier home where he found his mother on the phone with the police. Coldly and without any words, Christian raised the shotgun and fired once, killing his mother.

"There was no argument or quarrel of any kind," said Serge later about his brother's murders of their family members. "He just picked up his gun and fired it point blank at Corinne, killing her instantly. Then my mother telephoned the police . . . He fired and killed her too."

Many people who kill their family members in similar situations often stop there and turn the gun on themselves. But Christian Dornier hated the entire world and wanted everyone to pay for his miserable life, so he was not going to stop until someone made him.

After killing everyone he came in contact with at the Dornier home, Christian reloaded his gun and jumped into his car.

It was time to take his killing spree on the road.

Dornier drove his VW to Luxiol's city center to find some more victims. Almost immediately he came upon two young boys riding their bicycles around town, brothers Johan and Johnny Robez-Masson. He opened fire on the brothers, killing both instantly. He then drove a little further until he spotted Stanislas Pénard and his wife Marie strolling down the sidewalk, enjoying the warm summer day. The young couple never knew what hit them as the farm boy turned spree killer fired buckshot on both, which left them both dead on the street.

As Christian Dornier's body count quickly came to eight, another interesting fact about France's rural gun culture and the reality of gun culture in any country revealed itself.

The presence of more readily available guns may increase the odds of a mass shooting on the one hand, but on the other they can possibly limit the casualties in a mass shooting.

Dornier next shot and killed the mayor's five year-old niece who was standing in front of her home. The girl's father, who was standing nearby, shot back, hitting Dornier in the neck.

Wounded but not done killing, Dornier left Luxiol and drove on to the bigger town of Baume-les-Dames. In Baume-les-Dames, Dornier would claim five more lives, including a policeman named René Sarrazin. By the time Dornier's spree moved to Baume-les-Dames, forty policemen were following him through the town and then across the French countryside as the killer made his way for the town of Verne. Once he arrived in Verne, Dornier was met by even more police who shot him in the stomach, ending his sadistic spree across northeast France.

The final casualty count was fourteen dead, eight seriously wounded.

Insanity Defense

When the smoke finally cleared from Christian Dornier's shooting rampage, the authorities in the region decided to cancel Bastille Day celebrations. The citizens of Luxiol and Baume-les-Dames had wounded to take care of and dead to bury; the national holiday was the furthest thing from the minds of most area residents.

Dornier suffered life threatening injuries and was brought to a secure hospital where doctors fought to save the deranged shooter's life. The French spree killer was saved only to be charged with fourteen counts of murder and eight counts of attempted murder on July 15.

It seemed like an open and shut case for French prosecutors.

Christian Dornier was caught dead to rights. Multiple witnesses saw him at different points during the shooting spree and the farmer turned killer never tried to conceal his face. The French legal system may be thought of as lenient in some ways by American standards, but it was/is not in Europe.

France was one of the last Western European countries to abolish capital punishment. The preferred method of execution in France for over 200 years was the guillotine, which was last used on a criminal in 1977. The French government formally abolished capital punishment in 1981, making it one of the final countries now in the European Union to do so.

So Christian Dornier would not have to face the guillotine, but he very well could have been sent to a prison for the rest of his life.

France has a long history of notorious prisons where famous people, such as American revolutionary Patrick Henry, have languished for years. In more recent years the French government modernized their prison system, but long sentences are routinely handed down and many of the prisons are known for housing tough criminals and inmate gangs.

Christian Dornier would be a sitting duck in a French maximum security prison.

Dornier's defense attorneys knew that he would never be truly safe in a maximum security prison and that when, not if, he were convicted of the murders, he would be sent to such a prison for the remainder of his life.

They decided to try an insanity defense.

Attempts at insanity defenses are actually common during murder trials. A defendant with enough money will locate and pay mental health professionals who will testify that the defendant was insane when he/she committed the murder. Because of the possibility to abuse such a defense, most countries require an extremely high standard for someone to prove he/she was insane during the commission of a murder. The process involves separate hearings and the end result is that the judge usually rules the defendant competent to stand trial.

But sometimes the courts rule in favor of a defendant's insanity plea.

Investigators soon learned that Christian Dornier did indeed have mental health issues, had been to see a psychiatrist, and was prescribed medication. While Dornier was convalescing from his wounds in the hospital, the government sent its own team of psychiatrists to exam the shooter in order to determine if he could stand trial.

The psychiatrists reported that Christian Dornier suffered from schizophrenia and that he should not be held legally responsible for the July 12, 1989, rampage. Due to the findings, the French government sent Dornier to a state mental hospital on April 18, 1991, where he remains to this day.

Over the last twenty-five years, numerous petitions have been filed to have Dornier declared competent to stand trial in a criminal court; but all have been denied.

Christian Dornier's shooting spree truly upset the tranquility of the otherwise quiet French countryside. The rampage was the worst shooting in French history since a 1978 gangland shooting left ten people dead in Marseilles.

It took more than twenty-five years, but Dornier's carnage count was finally eclipsed by the November 2015 Paris terrorist attacks that left 130 people dead, over half from gunshots.

But the citizens of the quiet villages of northeast France will never forget Christian Dornier's shooting rampage.

CHAPTER 7:

THE MYSTERIOUS MURDER OF JESSICA LYNN KEEN

As discussed in an earlier chapter in this book, rebellion is a part of growing up and being a teenager. Most pass through the phase quickly and then move on with their lives. When most of us look back on our teen years, we often laugh at some of the things we did, while others may want to forget most of it.

Teen rebellion is handled by parents in a variety of different ways. Some parents give their insubordinate adolescents plenty of leeway, while others come down strongly on their recalcitrant kids. Parenting is not a "one size fits all" proposition and the best results seem to come from a variety of different methods.

But sometimes, no matter what a parent does, the worst case scenario will unfortunately happen.

A Good Girl Gone Bad

In 1991, Jessica Keen was a girl whose life took an interesting, difficult, and unexpected arc in her fifteen short years of life.

Jessica Keen grew up in the Weiland Park neighborhood of Columbus, Ohio, which is situated between the campus of Ohio State University and downtown Columbus. The neighborhood was fairly safe for a big city and she lived in a stable home. Her mother and father were married and living together and there was no abuse, drug use, or criminal activity taking place in the home.

Jessica got along well with her family and was popular at her high school. Her popularity in school translated into her being one of the top cheerleaders, but Jessica also excelled in academics and was an honor student. Jessica looked set to receive a scholarship from Ohio State University, or perhaps any number of universities.

But then eighteen-year-old bad boy Shawn Thompson came along.

The Keen parents immediately disliked Thompson, who they saw as lazy, shiftless, and lacking in any future. Thompson was also rumored to be involved in criminal activity in the area.

As Jessica's grades began to decline, the Keens' disapproval of their daughter's boyfriend became more adamant. They forbade her from seeing Thompson and then grounded her when she disobeyed them. Finally, feeling they were at their wit's end, the Keen parents made the drastic decision to send Jessica to a group home for troubled teens.

Jessica was sent to live in a nearby group home named the Huckleberry House on March 4, 1991. Her parents hoped that the exile would help to refocus Jessica on school and the future and if Thompson was unable to see her, so much the better.

Instead of helping their daughter, Jessica's sojourn to the group home proved to be her demise in a strange series of events that was only recently solved by modern science.

Jessica's Murder

On March 17, 1991, less than two weeks after she was sent to Huckleberry House, the naked body of Jessica Keen was discovered in a cemetery just outside of Columbus. The police quickly amassed a trail of physical evidence that painted a graphic image of Jessica's last minutes on earth.

Due to her naked body and duct tape on her hands and mouth, it became clear that Jessica had been abducted at some point on March 17. An autopsy revealed that she had been raped and beaten to death. A pendant she wore of the word "taken" was missing, but her watch and ring were left by the killer.

Investigators found one of Jessica's socks behind one gravestone and a knee imprint behind another. It became clear to homicide detectives that she escaped her attacker at some point and ironically, ran into the cemetery for refuge. She moved through the cemetery, hiding behind gravestones, until her devious killer finally caught her on the edge of the cemetery, which proved to be Jessica's final resting place.

The Keen family was mortified when they learned about Jessica's murder and the city of Columbus went into high alert when it was informed that a killer-rapist was roaming the streets freely.

The police quickly had a prime suspect—Jessica's boyfriend, Shawn Thompson

When investigators interviewed the staff and residents of the Huckleberry House, they learned that Jessica and Shawn had an argument on the phone on the night of March 17. After the phone call, Jessica signed out of the Huckleberry House around six pm and was never seen nor heard from again.

The Keen family and many in the city of Columbus thought that Shawn Thompson was good for the murder, but it was soon revealed that he could not have been the perpetrator. Thompson had witnesses who claimed he was on the way to Florida with them during the murder and DNA profiling, which still was still relatively new in the early 1990s, eventually proved him innocent.

Once Shawn Thompson was definitively ruled out as a suspect, the only thing left for the police to do was to store the biological evidence from the crime scene and hope that science would one day catch the killer.

Modern Science Reveals the Killer

As the 1990s started to go by, the parents of Jessica Keen and many of the investigators involved in her case began to lose hope that they would catch her killer. The young girl's brutal murder began to be featured less in local media stories, which was not due to her family's efforts. They routinely checked in with the local police and reporters in order to keep the case from going cold and to keep it in the minds of the public. Jessica's family's efforts were enough to get the case profiled on the popular American true-crime television show *Unsolved Mysteries* and was featured on an episode of *On the Case with Paula Zahn*. Despite these efforts, it looked to many as though Jessica's killer would never be caught.

In the years since Jessica's murder, the science of DNA profiling advanced rapidly.

The biological samples taken from Jessica's body were preserved in a crime lab and then entered into the Combined DNA Index System (CODIS) when Ohio became part of the database in the 2000s. When Congress passed the DNA Identification Act in 1994, it cleared the way for the creation of a nationwide DNA base of convicted criminals. Although CODIS is an FBI program, samples are taken from offenders in all fifty states, the federal government, and the District of Colombia. At first, samples were taken from convicted sex offenders in various states, but over the years the database has grown to include persons convicted of all felonies and in some states, those even charged with felonies and some misdemeanors. Each individual state determines its own criteria for who is required to give DNA samples, but by 2006 every state had joined the CODIS database on some level.

Columbus police suspected that whoever killed Jessica had either committed a serious crime before, or would again at some point. In 2008 the investigators theory proved to be true when they received a match in the CODIS system for the semen left on Jessica's body.

The sample belonged to a man named Marvin Lee Smith Junior. It was immediately clear that Smith's sample was no fluke: he was a career criminal who was out on bond for sexually assaulting two Columbus women when Jessica was murdered. On April 9, 2008, Columbus police traveled to North Carolina and arrested Smith for the murder of Jessica.

Once Smith was extradited to Ohio to stand trial for capital murder in 2009, he showed his cowardly nature by pleading guilty to the murder in order to avoid the death penalty. As part of a plea bargain that got him a life sentence instead of the needle, Smith was required to tell the court what happened the night of Jessica's murder.

Coming off the previous two sexual assaults, the depraved Smith was driven to rape again, but this time he had to make sure his victim could not go to the police. As he drove around Columbus looking for his next victim, he spied Jessica waiting alone at a bus stop. Like a true predator, Smith pulled up next to Jessica, assaulted her, and then threw her into his car. He then bound her with duct tape and raped the frightened girl. Jessica apparently knew that her attacker had no plans to let her live, so she ran from the car into the cemetery. Smith admitted that he had a difficult time finding her in the graveyard, but he was helped when Jessica unwittingly ran into a fencepost, which knocked her unconscious.

The killer then finished Jessica off by smashing a tombstone over her head.

The cold irony of being murdered in a cemetery is something that is difficult to contemplate and will always live with Jessica's parents.

"I can still feel Jessica's heart beating as she ran for her life that day," said Jessica's mother, Rebecca Smitley. "I can see her hiding behind tombstones and I can hear her praying.

CHAPTER 8:

MATTIAS FLINK'S SWEDISH SHOOTING SPREE

Since the 1970s, the focus of the justice system in most industrialized countries has been to rehabilitate, instead of just punishing criminals, or at least that is what is said. Prisons and jails in many countries offer classes to inmates ranging from parenting to vocational and college courses that are aimed at helping inmates find jobs after they are released.

The old days of locking someone up and throwing away the keys are long over.

Despite the emphasis on rehabilitation over punishment, modern justice systems still function to punish those who have ran afoul of society's laws. The very act of separating a person from his family, friends, and greater society is an act of punishment and few will argue that in countries that still have the death penalty, the execution of a criminal is an act of revenge on behalf of the victims' families and society itself.

Lengthy prison sentences handed out to murderers are viewed by most as the proper course for a person who has committed the ultimate crime. Proponents of long prison sentences argue that such sentences protect society from convicted murderers, who may kill again, and also serve to punish the most heinous offenders.

But how does society determine if a killer is truly reformed? Even if a killer is said to be reformed, should he continue to be held as punishment for his crime(s) as revenge for the victims?

These are common questions that are often bandied about by legal scholars who seek to create the most fair justice system. In the United States, convicted murderers usually serve very long prison sentences for one murder and it is unheard for a spree or serial killer to ever obtain parole.

Things are a bit different in Scandinavia.

Since crime is relatively low in the Scandinavian countries, their justice systems have funding for more expansive inmate rehabilitation programs. The prisons in Norway, Sweden, and Denmark, are viewed by many in corrections as models for the industrialized world and sentencing for crimes is often creative and lenient, at least by American standards.

For instance, a true life sentence is unheard of in most Scandinavian countries. This point was particularly made clear to the world when Norwegian terrorist Anders Breivik was sentenced to twenty-one years "preventive detention" in Norway for his attack that left seventy seven people dead and over 300 wounded. Under the law, the government can imprison Breivik indefinitely, but he will also be eligible for parole after ten years. Most experts say the chance that Breivik will ever be released are remote, but one only has to look at neighboring Sweden and the case of Mattias Flink to know that when it comes to remote probabilities in Scandinavian justice systems, one should not discount anything.

Mattias Flink killed seven people and injured one in what many consider to be Sweden's worst crime.

The convicted spree killer was recently released from prison!

The Mattias Flink murder spree raised alarms and anger in the liberal, peaceful Nordic nation that had not witnessed that type of violence since the Vikings made Scandinavia their home. A frenzy of media attention gripped Sweden in the months following Flink's murder spree in 1994 and years later when the case became the center of attention again as Flink fought to be released from prison.

Mattias Flink

Mattias Flink was born on March 8, 1970, to a middle-class family in the small central Swedish town of Falun. From an early age Flink was surrounded by guns because his father worked as a gunsmith. Although handguns are severely restricted in Sweden, rifles and shotguns are quite common and the country is usually in the ten top of the countries with the most guns per 100 residents.

Mattias' father showed him how to properly care for and maintain firearms around the house and the two would also often do target practice together.

The Flink home was stable; the father earned enough to support the small family and there was no abuse. Despite the early stability of the Flink home, his parents came under the same stresses that most families experience in modern industrialized countries, which ended in divorce when Mattias was nine.

Psychiatrists point to his parents' divorce as an early traumatic and defining experience in Mattias Flink's life.

After the divorce was finalized, young Mattias stayed in the family home with his father while his mother moved down the street. He began to resent his mother for the divorce.

He began to resent women for everything!

For the most part, Flink's youth was rather non-descript. He had few friends and spent most of his time around the family home until he graduated from high school and then joined the Swedish army.

Army life seemed to agree with Flink as it gave him some things that were otherwise missing in his life. The rules gave him order, discipline, and direction that were not there before and although he still maintained a reasonable personal distance from the other soldiers, he did develop a sense of comradery with officers and enlisted men alike.

Flink's dedication to military life eventually paid off when he was promoted the rank of Second Lieutenant. It looked to many of Flink's family and long-time friends that the young man had finally found his place in life and was truly happy.

Looks can be deceiving.

The entire time that Flink was being promoted through the ranks of the Swedish military, his hatred for the world kept festering. Although he had a girlfriend in 1994, Flink increasingly began to shut her and all of his other acquaintances out from his inner circle that only included Mattias Flink.

In the first couple months of 1994 Flink also began drinking heavily. The drinking combined with his misanthropic nature led to him acting aggressively on numerous occasions towards friends and acquaintances, as he accused them of conspiring against him.

The signs were all there: heavy drinking, isolation, and paranoia;

but no one, including his superiors at the army base, believed there was a problem.

They would all soon find out just how much of a problem Mattias Flink could be!

Washing Falun in Blood

Falun is a sleepy college town of about 40,000 people located in the central part of Sweden. Once one of the of primary producers of iron and copper in Europe, by early 1994 more of Falun's residents were employed in the educational, recreational, and military sectors than in mining.

The military presence in Falun was barely considered by the local residents before 1994, partly because it had been there so long, but also because incidents of criminal behavior that have a tendency to follow military bases were for the most part absent.

Until June 11, 1994.

June 11 began like many other days for Mattias Flink. It was just another day—another day for him to hate the world. But unlike those other days, Flink would do something about it on this day.

Flink began the day drinking copious amounts of hard liquor, which only served to harden his already negative disposition. At some point during his drinking binge, Flink began to argue with his girlfriend. The argument seemed to flip a switch in Flink's twisted mind, but for some reason he never laid a hand on his girlfriend.

Perhaps he wanted her to see the carnage that he was capable of.

Flink finished of a bottle of vodka, got dressed, and then loaded his military issued AK 5 rifle.

He then headed for the park to hunt his game—women!

Flink could not have picked a better time to hunt women in Fulan because when he arrived at the park, a squad of the Sweden Women's Auxiliary Service was conducting drills. Eyeing up his hated quarry, Flink fired several shots from his high-powered rifle into the crowd of women, killing five and injuring one.

Flink then surveyed the situation and noticed a man on a bicycle had just witnessed the shooting, so he shot and killed him. An unarmed security guard who was on duty nearby ran to the vicinity to help out, but he was also shot and killed by the woman-hating gunman.

With eight bullet-ridden bodies strewn across the park, Flink then ran from the area to a nearby construction site to hide.

It is unknown if Flink was seriously trying to hide from the police or if he was merely catching his breath before he killed more people: he left his house with 150 rounds of ammo and barely used any of them during his proficient killing spree in the park. But the local police were on high alert and soon two officers spotted Flink in his makeshift hideout. A shootout ensued that left Flink with a bullet in the hip and in handcuffs.

The killing spree in Falun was over, but the legal saga of Mattias Flink had just begun.

Life In and Out of Prison

Perhaps "saga" is the most appropriate word in this case and best sums up the trial, conviction, imprisonment, and eventual release of Mattias Flink. Saga is after all an Old Norse word for the stories about the Viking kings and jarls who at one time ruled over Sweden. Most sagas followed a standard formula: the protagonist loses his birthright for some reason and is then forced to endure tribulations before returning home and claiming what is rightfully his, usually through acts of extreme violence. Now Flink never had any claim to nobility and the tribulations he endured were largely the result of mental health issues, but the legal maneuvering connected to his trial and imprisonment represent a saga of a different sort.

Flink was immediately charged with murder in a case that was sensationalized in the Swedish media, but it was also a case that most saw as open and shut. Plenty of witnesses saw Flink shoot numerous people and then there was that shootout he got into with the police.

But never underestimate a good defense lawyer!

At first, it seemed as though Sweden's low crime rate might work to Flink's advantage because his attorneys were able to use a defense that was previously unknown in Sweden—not guilty due to an alcohol induced psychosis.

The defense that "alcohol made me do it" may seem laughable today, but in 1994 Flink's lawyers considered it a legitimate defense. Low crime rates and a liberal justice system meant that Swedish judges and juries were more apt to consider such a defense as opposed to their American counterparts who are more cynical due to high crime rates.

After all, a nice solider like Mattias Flink certainly had to be out of his mind to commit such terrible crimes, right?

Despite well-reasoned arguments by the defense, the court rejected Flink's claims of insanity by the bottle and found him guilty of murder. Not only was Flink's booze defense rejected in his trial, it created a nationwide precedent so that criminal defendants cannot use the "so drunk I'm insane" defense in Sweden today.

Once Flink was convicted and sentenced to life in prison, the people of Sweden thought they had heard the last of the butcher of Falun. Little did they know that it was really just the beginning of the next chapter in the saga of Mattias Flink.

Like most people serving an extended sentence behind bars, Flink was moved to a couple of different prisons. For the most part, he was well behaved, but he kept to himself. Because of a combination of his misanthropic attitude and the notoriety of his crime, Flink was unpopular with the other inmates. Despite the other inmates' hatred of Flink, he was able to avoid any serious assaults at their hands.

Flink put his solitude behind bars to good use.

The spree killer took part in prison rehabilitation programs and showed enough promise to prison staff that he was allowed furloughs starting in 2007, despite serving a life sentence. The shooter of Falun also used his time to study Swedish law and legal procedures and learned that he had an outside chance of reducing his sentence.

Beginning in 2008, Flink filed numerous appeals with the courts to have his sentence reduced from life to twenty-four years. Once the media learned of Flink's legal maneuvering, the rampage in Falun became headlines once more and the people of Sweden became outraged that such a heinous killer may once again roam their streets.

In 2010, the Norns began to favor Flink in a series of court rulings. An appeals court agreed to reduce Flink's sentence to thirty-two years, but then a subsequent ruling handed him thirty-six years. Finally, Sweden's Supreme Court handed Flink an adjusted sentence of thirty years, which gave the spree killer a parole date of June 11, 2014, exactly twenty years after he gunned down seven people in Falun.

Since his release from prison, Flink's identity and location have been kept secret from the public. It remains to be seen if Flink was truly rehabilitated by his prison experience; perhaps he got the help he needed. To many of the family members of Flink's victims the question of his rehabilitation is a moot point. To victims' families, he should stay in prison for the rest of his life for punishment, if nothing else.

Only time will tell what happens next.

Is there another chapter waiting to be written in the strange saga of Mattias Flink?

CHAPTER 9:

MATTHEW TVRDON'S WHITE VAN RAMPAGE

In recent years, automobiles have been used quite frequently around the world as weapons. One does not have to search the Internet very long to find examples of this. The 2002 case of Clara Harris repeatedly running over her husband in a parking lot is one of the more striking cases. As in the Clara Harris case, most automobile homicides are very personal and directed at only one or two people, so the casualty count tends to be low.

Make no mistake, an automobile can be just as deadly in the wrong hands as a gun, knife, or bomb.

Unfortunately, the world was starkly shown this reality when a terrorist plowed a truck into a crowd of Bastille Day revelers in Nice, France, killing dozens.

But before the Bastille Day truck attack in Nice, there was Matthew Tvrdon and his white van rampage in Cardiff, Wales!

The Death Van

Wales is an interesting country. A trip through the rural mountain country of Wales will demonstrate to anyone that despite being a part of the United Kingdom, Wales is indeed a unique place. Many of the people still speak their native Welsh language and the names of the country's cities, lakes, and mountains also retain their incredibly long and difficult to pronounce Welsh names, although many locals admit that it would be easier to use English names. Despite holding strong to their cultural traditions, most Welsh are happy being part of the Kingdom and do not display the vehement and sometimes violent anti-English attitude often seen in Northern Ireland and Scotland.

Wales is truly a quiet and charming country.

At least it was until twenty-nine-year-old Matthew Tvrdon filled up his van with gas on October 19, 2012 and decided to turn that vehicle into a lethal weapon.

Matthew Tvrdon was an average guy in many ways. He worked an average job at a government tax office, but eventually the stress of dealing with other people's money became too much and he had a nervous breakdown.

Or perhaps there were problems all along.

Tvrdon's behavior at work earned him an extended stay at a Cardiff psychiatric hospital, but he was allowed to return to his job after he was released from the hospital. After his return to work, it soon became apparent to his co-workers that the stay in the hospital did not help and if anything, Tvrdon seemed even more withdrawn.

Most people who knew Tvrdon before his rampage had good things to say about him and one co-worker even stated that their employer "seriously let him down" by not taking his mental health more seriously.

Matthew Tvrdon's neighbors from the neighborhood he grew up in also had good things to say about the killer. He was known to be polite and enjoyed working on cars, either alone or with his father or two younger brothers.

There was no abuse in the Tvrdon home and the parents were not involved in criminal activity, drug use, or heavy drinking. It seemed a mystery how a well-adjusted boy could transform into a mental basket-case by the age of thirty.

Perhaps he was a spurned lover?

Tvrdon was dating an older forty-six-year-old woman in the months before his rampage, but the woman was said to have broken off the relationship. It is unknown what role this may have played, but authorities have down played it.

The world may never know the true intentions of Tvrdon's murderous spree, but the citizens of Cardiff continue to live with its repercussions.

It all began on a Friday afternoon at 3:30 pm. Children had been let out of school and many of their parents were there to pick up them. The streets of Cardiff were alive with the sounds of children laughing.

Within minutes the laughs turned to screams.

After Tvrdon checked his van one last time, he made his way to the Ely and Leckwith districts to find some victims. He did not have to wait long.

Tvrdon immediately went into action, driving his van into groups of adults and children wherever he could find them. He swerved across several lanes of traffic in order to attack one group and then back to the other side of the street to run over a couple who were walking their baby in a stroller.

The psychotic van driver plowed into the couple, thrusting the child several feet into the air. Somehow the child lived!

Tvrdon then drove up the street to a local fire department station where he spied thirty-one-year old mother Karina Menzies and her two children. Menzies, who had problems walking because of a degenerative disease, had her infant with her as she had just picked up her eight-year-old from school. As the white van of death sped towards Menzies, the mother did the only thing possible and threw her two children to safety.

The white van crushed Menzies' body, killing her instantly.

By the time Karina Menzies was killed, Tvrdon had already hit and driven over at least a dozen people, so the police were on their way.

Street-beat cops in the United Kingdom are known world-wide for not carrying firearms, but firearms and other weapons are available if needed.

And the Cardiff police needed some heavy power to take down Matthew Tvrdon!

After Tvrdon killed Menzies, the white van rampage soon turned into a hot pursuit as dozens of local police gave chase to the crazed killer.

Tvrdon led the Cardiff Police on a chase that went for several miles through several neighborhoods and finally ended when the police shot tear gas into the killer's car.

The white van rampage was over.

The Sentence

Once Tvrdon was captured and placed in custody, he faced the anger of a nation and the possibility that he would spend the rest of his life in prison. The case was never a "who done it?" Numerous closed circuit television cameras captured the carnage and were able to corroborate witnesses who saw and survived the mayhem. The real question concerned whether or not Tvrdon was legally responsible for his actions or if he was insane.

After a number of pre-trial hearings intended to determine Tvrdon's sanity, a judge ruled that the killer was not criminally responsible because, like Christian Dornier, he suffered from schizophrenia. In 2013, Tvrdon was then sentenced to an indefinite term at a maximum security mental hospital.

Many of the people at the hearing, who were also survivors of the van attack, became irate and yelled their disapproval of the sentence to the judge, press, and anyone else who would listen. As one man left the courtroom he shouted, "They should have put a gun to his head." Of course the statement was hyperbole and more than likely just a way for a frustrated person to blow off steam since the death penalty was abolished during the 1960s in the United Kingdom.

Despite what many may think, Matthew Tvrdon did not get off lightly.

Experts say that he will probably spend the rest of his life at the Ashworth high-security hospital, which is located in the northwest English town of Merseyside. The hospital is little better than an average British prison in most ways and the "indefinite" sentence does not mean that he will ever be released.

Once the sentence was handed down the judge made sure to add, "However, you should expect that you will be detained for a very long time."

Matthew Tvrdon will most likely never terrorize the streets of Cardiff, or any other city in the United Kingdom.

CHAPTER 10:

THE CASE OF THE REAL LIFE ZOMBIE, TYREE SMITH

Zombie movies and television shows have become the rage over the last few years. The success of *The Walking Dead* television show has led to numerous imitators on cable television and a plethora of movies and books that are too numerous to count.

Truly, the world has become obsessed with zombies.

For most people, becoming immersed in a world overrun with flesh eating undead creatures is more of an escape from the mundane nature of daily life more than anything else. We find satisfaction when our favorite hero or heroine escapes the clutches of a pack of flesh eaters in the latest episode of our favorite zombie show and we are perhaps even happier to watch the villains eviscerated by zombies. Once the show is over though, it is back to reality and the daily grind.

But some people among us have a desire for human flesh and the most disturbed of those people sometimes act on those desires.

All throughout history there have been reports of people who have broken mankind's biggest taboo—cannibalism. With that said, reports of cannibalism have been rare enough that they are usually well reported and often under understandable circumstances. For instance, Russian civilians who were trapped in Stalingrad during that city's siege by the Germans in late 1942 and early 1943 were said to have survived by eating dead friends and family members. And of course there is the famous case of the Uruguayan rugby team whose plane crashed in the Andes Mountains in 1972. The surviving members of the team were able to survive by eating the bodies of the dead.

Those were true cases of life and death, where the survivors had to eat human flesh and by all accounts found the act extremely difficult.

Then there are truly disturbed people who enjoy eating human flesh, like Ed Gein. Ed Gein made international headlines when it was discovered that the central Wisconsin farmer had killed and eaten some of his neighbors. The world was disturbed that not only was Gein a murderer, but also a cannibal who hid among his neighbors in plain sight.

Nearly sixty years later, a cannibal named Tyree Smith struck on the streets of Bridgeport, Connecticut, raising alarm in the city. Some of the older residents were reminded of the Ed Gein case decades earlier, but most people, influenced by the current zombie rage, saw Smith as a true-to-life zombie.

Eyeballs Taste Like Oysters

In January 2012, thirty-four-year-old Tyree Smith was just another person who fell through the cracks. Smith had spent his life in and out of correctional and mental health facilities and dealing with substance abuse issues. He had a difficult time finding good paying work and when he did find a job he was usually fired fairly quickly. As he got older, Smith became increasingly estranged from his family and was often homeless.

Life had been tough for Tyree Smith.

On January 20, 2012, Smith found himself homeless in the middle of a Connecticut winter and desperately needed a place to stay and keep warm. After searching around the city for a place to crash, Smith found what looked like a vacant house and quickly fell asleep on the porch due to exhaustion.

After sleeping for a couple of hours, Smith was woken up by a man who invited him inside to sleep. The man was not the home's owner; Smith was correct that the house was vacant. The stranger was forty-three-year-old homeless drifter Angel Gonzalez.

There is no evidence that Gonzalez tried to do anything violent to Smith, or that he may made an unwanted sexual advance. It appears that Smith simply snapped in order to satiate his unnatural taste for human flesh.

Not long after moving his things into the house, Smith pulled out an axe and hacked Gonzalez to death. The motiveless murder was bizarre in its own right, but what happened next was just incredibly weird.

Smith surveyed his victim and then proceeded to remove an eyeball and some of the brain matter. He then left the body in the vacant house but took the eyeball and brain matter to a family member's grave at a nearby cemetery. Smith then ate the eyeball, which "tasted like an oyster," according to his arrest warrant. He also chowed down on the brain matter.

Smith then went on the run for a few days but was arrested on January 24 in Florida.

After Smith was extradited back to Connecticut, the details of his bizarre, horrific crime became public.

Smith showed up at the home of his cousin, Nicole Rabb, the day before the murder and zombie feast. Rabb testified that he acted stranger than normal and that he was "talking about Greek gods and ruminating about needing to go out and get blood."

Instead of blood, Smith got an eyeball and some brain matter.

In pre-trial hearings it became obvious to both the defense and prosecutor that Smith was not sane. A three judge panel agreed and declared the zombie killer not guilty by reason of insanity in July 2013. Technically, the ruling meant that the panel could have ordered his immediate release because he was ruled not-guilty. But the ruling also made Smith a ward of the state until he is deemed no longer a danger to himself or anyone else, so it seems likely that the zombie killer will be spending quite a while, if not the rest of his life, in a state hospital.

"It is overwhelmingly clear that his discharge from custody would constitute a danger to himself and others," stated Superior Court Judge John Kavenewsky as he ordered Smith to sixty years confinement in a secured mental hospital.

Although most in attendance seemed to think that the lengthy confinement in a mental hospital was a fair resolution for the strange crime, some of Gonzalez's family still had a difficult time coming to grips with the bizarre circumstances of Angel's murder.

"Here it is that my dad was trying to help this guy, telling him to come inside from the cold," said Odalys Vazquez, a daughter of

Angel Gonzalez. "If my father was helping him stay warm, what kind of person is it who does this—who repays him by swinging an axe at him and hitting him so hard it blows his brains out?"

It was a legitimate question, but the circumstances surrounding this case are just so strange that Tyree Smith himself will probably never be able to answer it, at least not in a way that normal people would understand.

CHAPTER 11:

THE COLD MURDER CASE OF WILHELMINA AND ED MAURIN

There are usually many reasons why a murder case becomes cold. A lack of physical evidence, motive, or suspects are always problems that can stymie an investigation, but oftentimes there is a lack of will and resources to solve many of these murders. Police departments are forced to budget their resources, which includes manpower, so some cases get temporarily pushed aside while attention is given to more pressing cases. Unfortunately, the cases that are often temporarily pushed aside are usually forgotten about by investigators. The lack of urgency is even more apparent when a considerable amount of time has elapsed since the crime.

Investigators are transferred, promoted, and retire, which means that twenty or thirty years after a murder has been committed and the case has grown cold, there are few if any investigators around who worked on the case originally.

The will to capture the perpetrators of cold case murders often comes from friends and family members of the victims. It is their efforts that keep the cold cases in the public eye through the media, as well as by constantly keeping contact with law enforcement assigned to solve the crimes.

The 1985 cold case murders of eighty-three-year-old Wilhelmina "Winnie" Maurin and her eighty-one-year-old husband Ed is a perfect example of a family member not giving up and ultimately making sure that their murder did not remain cold.

"At their funeral, I laid my hand on their casket," said Dennis Hadaller, the son of Winnie and Ed Maurin. "I said, I will find out who did this."

Eventually, Dennis' persistence paid off—nearly thirty years later—but not before the case took some twists and turns.

A Brutal Murder

Winnie and Ed Maurin were discovered shot to death in the woods outside of Centralia, Washington on Christmas Eve, 1985. The brutality and apparent randomness of the murders perplexed the residents of Lewis County, Washington. Lewis County is predominately rural, has fewer than 100,000 residents, and is known for its low crime rates.

The crime scene, or perhaps dumping scene, indicated that their deaths were no accident. Whoever it was they met up with, that person or persons intended to kill the Maurins.

With plenty of questions, but few leads, the Lewis County Sherriff's Department got to work creating a chronology of the Maurins' last days alive. They started with the date when the Maurin's were last seen or heard from.

December 19, 1985, was an important date for the Maurin family. That night, the extended Maurin family was supposed to meet at Winnie and Ed's home to celebrate Christmas, but when the guests began to arrive they found the Maurin home locked and totally dark.

Feeling that something was wrong, Dennis and some of his other relatives went to the Lewis County Sherriff's Department to file a missing person report. The Sherriff's department quickly determined that the Maurins were not a couple trying to get lost and that they had both either succumbed to some type of affliction common in old age—Alzheimer's disease, heart attack, or stroke just to name three possibilities—or they met with untimely demises at the hands of others.

An extensive search was conducted throughout Lewis County, which turned up the Maurins' car the next day.

The discovery of the Maurins' car was greeted with optimism by the Maurin family, but that hope soon faded when they learned about the conditions of the interior: the key was still in the ignition and there was a lot of blood on the seats.

So much blood, investigators said, that if it were shed by even two people they most surely died of blood loss. The Maurin family's hopes of finding Winnie and Ed alive sunk and were permanently dashed when the bodies of the elderly couple were discovered on Christmas Eve.

The disappearance of Winnie and Ed Maurin was officially ruled a double homicide and local investigators immediately set to work finding their killers.

But they soon found out how difficult a homicide investigation can be without physical evidence.

Two Suspects Emerge

Smaller law enforcement agencies in the United States, such as the Lewis County Sherriff's Department, are often underfunded and therefore do not often have the latest crime fighting technologies that bigger departments possess. The smaller tax bases in less populated towns and counties is one of the primary reasons these departments have less resources, but these communities also tend to have less of a need because crime rates are traditionally lower in these locations.

And all of the latest technologies would not have helped much anyway.

Investigators were immediately faced with the problem of a lack of physical evidence at the crime scene. Although DNA profiling was unknown in 1985, investigators could test blood for types and the only types they could identify from the car were those that matched Ed's and Winnie's. There were also no fingerprints other than the Maurins in the car or their home. Closed circuit television cameras were a fairly novel concept in 1985 and there were few witnesses that could help investigators, at least in the early stages of the investigation.

Ed Maurin was seen in Chehalis under strange circumstances on the day of the 19th.

The investigators were able to combine the Ed Maurin sighting with tips from informants to not only zero in on two suspects, but also to recreate the horrific crime that took the lives of two innocent people.

In 1985, Rick and John Riffe were a couple of twenty-somethings with no real ambitions or plans for the future. Although the two brothers were known to local law enforcement as bottom of the totem pole criminals, they were not known to have been especially violent or to have committed any major crimes, so they stayed under police radars for the most part.

But when the Lewis County Sherriff's Department began hearing stories that the two were involved in the murder of the Maurins, they began to take notice.

As the police built a case against the two brothers, the Riffes moved up to Alaska. Younger brother John died in 2012, so he evaded justice on this earth, but in 2013 Rick was charged for the murders of Winnie and Ed Maurin.

Behind the efforts to charge the one surviving brother was Dennis Hadaller, who hired a private investigator in the early 2000s. The private investigator revealed new witnesses, which ultimately helped police piece together the crime and charge Rick Riffe with murder.

According to the police and the Lewis County prosecutor's office, the murder of the Maurins was purely financially based. An employee at the Sterling Savings and Loan banks in Chehalis testified that a man whose voice she did not recognize called around closing time on December 18, 1985 and asked if it were too late to withdraw a large sum of cash. The teller told the man to call back the next day.

The mysterious caller never gave his name. The next day the same teller got a call about withdrawing a large sum of cash, but this time it was from a customer she knew: Ed Maurin.

Ed arrived at the bank promptly at 10:30 am on the morning of the 19th and withdrew $8,500 in $100 bills. He told the teller that he needed the money in order to buy a new car. When the teller asked about Winnie, who usually accompanied Ed into the bank, he replied that she was not feeling well and decided to wait in the car. The teller told Ed that they did not have that much money on hand and that he would have to wait for more cash to arrive. Ed decided to wait in his car with his wife.

After Ed finally got his cash, he thanked the teller and told her that he would drive his new car through the drive-up window the next time he came to the bank.

That was the last time Ed was seen alive.

Police theorize that the Riffe brothers had picked the Maurins as marks days or weeks before the homicides were committed. Rick gained entry to the Maurin home in the early morning hours of the 19th and then forced the couple at gunpoint into their 1969 Chrysler. John then joined his brother and the four drove into town together to get Ed's money.

The Maurins' car was spotted several times around town that day, including driving away from the Maurin home with all four occupants.

Based on the autopsy of Ed, one or both of the brothers hit the elderly man at least twice on the top of the head in order to get him to comply. They then threatened to kill Winnie if Ed did not withdraw the money and they waited with her in the car as insurance.

Although robbery was the primary intent of the plot, the Riffe brothers probably intended to kill their marks from the beginning. They were loose ends that needed to be cut.

Dead men tell no tales!

But Rick Riffe learned that although dead men might not be able to tell tales, living witnesses can. Riffe's attorney argued that since his client's fingerprints and DNA were not found at the crime scene, then there was no way a jury could convict beyond a reasonable doubt. He also pointed out that some of the eyewitness testimony conflicted.

But the witnesses whose testimony did not conflict with others were considered credible and the circumstances of the situation proved to be too much. A Lewis County, Washington jury convicted Rick Riffe of murder on November 19, 2013.

Despite a lack of physical evidence, Lewis County Sheriff Steve Mansfield never doubted the Riffe brothers' guilt in the murders.

"I believe in karma, these are bad, evil people," Mansfield said.

CHAPTER 12:

THE 1993 LONG ISLAND RAILWAY SHOOTING RAMPAGE

Recently, many Western countries have been plagued with high profile mass shootings. Islamic extremists killed dozens of people in shooting attacks in Paris, France, in 2015 and 2016 and in the American cities of San Bernardino, California in 2015 and Orlando, Florida in 2016. There have also been some high profile shootings driven by racial and political animosity: a shooting of a predominately black church in Charleston, South Carolina, by a white supremacist and the recent shootings of multiple police officers in Dallas, Texas and Baton Rouge, Louisiana by black supremacists demonstrate that unfortunately sometimes people with axes to grind turn to violence for their solutions.

Before there were these most recent attacks, there was Colin Ferguson.

Colin Ferguson was a Jamaican immigrant who blamed others for his own inability to attain the American dream. Whites were the recipients of the majority of his vitriol, but Asians and blacks that he believed conspired with whites against him were also among his enemies. For years Ferguson ruminated about his pathetic existence and how he would one day exact his revenge against those who wronged him.

On December 7, 1993, Ferguson's rage boiled over when he took revenge on a Long Island rail car of innocent commuters, who wronged the man by merely existing because they happened to be white or Asian. When the smoke cleared, Ferguson's rampage of hate claimed six lives and left seventeen others wounded, some permanently.

Colin Ferguson's Early Life

Colin Ferguson was born on January 14, 1958, to a successful, affluent family in Jamaica. Growing up as a privileged Jamaican, Ferguson attended some of the best schools in the country and excelled in academics and sports such as cricket and soccer.

To anyone who knew Ferguson during his childhood, it seemed highly unlikely that the boy would grow up to become a notorious spree killer. He came from a stable family, received a good education, and showed no signs of violent tendencies towards animals or other children.

But as some of the other cases profiled in this book can attest to, there are usually problems underneath the façade of the public persona.

The young Ferguson was said to be spoiled and as he got older he came to expect a certain standard of living. Everything changed, though, when both his parents died in the late 1970s and he was left to fend for himself.

Broke and with no prospects in Jamaica, he came to the United States in 1982 on a tourist visa in order to game the system.

Most foreigners who enter the United States on a tourist visa are only allowed to stay for ninety days and are not permitted to work. If one overstays the visa, or finds work, then that person is subject to deportation.

Ferguson thought that the rules did not apply to him, so he overstayed his visa and looked for a full-time job. Since he did not have the proper work permits from the government, Ferguson was unable to find work other than menial labor.

Colin Ferguson was used to getting things his way in Jamaica, which in his mind meant that if things did not go his way in the United States forces must be at work against him. He began to blame the government, especially whites in the government, for his perceived problems. The fact that he simply did not follow the rules did not matter to the spree killer. He also took everything personally and began to believe that whites were conspiring against him personally.

But he knew that he could not keep the Immigration and Naturalization Service off his back forever and he also knew that if he were to get ahead in the United States, despite the racists he believed were out to get him, then he needed to get a green card.

To remedy the situation he did what thousands of others in his situation have done before and after: he married an American citizen!

Ferguson received permanent status to reside in the United States when he married Audrey Warren in 1986. It appears that the marriage was actually legitimate, at least to begin with, as the two stayed married until 1988. According to people who knew Ferguson during that time, the divorce from Warren shattered the Jamaican's already fragile ego. He became more withdrawn and although he still harbored an intense animosity towards whites, he began to focus his anger on women as well.

Somehow, despite his questionable resident status and his diminishing mental state, he found work as a security guard near his home on Long Island, New York. He was fired when he was injured on the job, which led to his first battle against the system in the form of a lawsuit from which he later won a settlement.

Instead of sitting around and waiting for his settlement, Ferguson enrolled in classes at Nassau Community College and actually showed some academic promise. He did well in all of his classes and made the Dean's List; but it was becoming increasingly difficult for Ferguson to hide his hatred and mental instability.

The Jamaican ex-pat began to argue with his professors and constantly injected race into class discussions, even when it was not remotely related to the topic at hand. His arguments with the professors became more heated and loud until he finally threatened violence on at least one occasion.

Threats of violence are taken extremely seriously on American college campuses, so Ferguson was expelled from Nassau Community College.

The Transition to a Race Warrior

A rational person would realize that threatening your professor will never turn out well.

But Colin Ferguson was not a rational person!

He let his hatred for whites stew while he sat alone in his apartment. He watched as whites drove down the street in new cars and he saw the nice new homes they lived in as took his daily ride on the train. Surely, Ferguson thought, the only reason why he did not have those things is because they were all out to get him.

Ferguson knew that his world view was correct and that if he were given the proper forum then others would agree, so after his expulsion from Nassau Community College, he transferred to the nearby Adelphi University in 1990.

After he transferred to Adelphi, Ferguson believed that he would meet others who were sympathetic to his increasingly extreme views. He began to speak openly in his classes of his contempt for whites and accused a female classmate of hurling racial epithets at him in the library.

The accusations proved to be false.

Ferguson then went to an anti-Apartheid symposium on the college campus, hoping to meet some fellow black radicals. Instead, he was angered to learn that the symposium allowed in whites and that the blacks conducting it were little more than "Uncle Toms" in Ferguson's twisted mind.

Alvin Makepela, a black African professor who helped sponsor the event, later told reporters about his run in with Ferguson during the symposium.

According to Makepela, Ferguson shouted from the audience and interrupted a scheduled speaker, saying, "We should be talking about the revolution in South Africa and how to get rid of the whites." The professor then exhorted Ferguson to let the speaker finish.

"You are one of those black people who have been employed at Adelphi to make sure black people don't succeed," was Ferguson's illogical response.

Ferguson continued with his racially tinged verbal tirades at Adelphi until the administration finally washed their hands of him with a suspension in June 1991.

For the next year and a half, Ferguson bounced from job to job, but he dedicated most of his time to the war he was to planning to bring to Long Island.

Colin Ferguson's Race War

Ferguson planned for his war by first legally buying a nine millimeter semi-automatic pistol and over 100 rounds of nine millimeter hollow point bullets. Hollow point bullets usually cause more destruction when they enter a human body because once they hit a bone they usually splinter into several pieces.

The shooter next had to find a target.

A mass shooting is one of the easiest terrorist attacks to plan and execute. The act can be done alone and it only requires a large crowd of people. In Ferguson's case the crowd needed to be white, but if some Asians and Hispanics were in the crowd that would be fine with him. Since he was living in Brooklyn right before he carried out his attack, Ferguson had access to plenty of targets in around Manhattan where plenty of white and Asian tourists would have been on hand.

But Ferguson's war was just as much a personal one as it was motivated by race and politics. Ferguson believed that his failures in life were caused by whites who were out to get him *personally*. Because of that, he decided to kill plenty of whites who wronged him in Long Island.

He decided that the daily commuter train that ran between the city and the Long Island suburbs would be the perfect location. It was crowded with plenty of whites, some of whom probably wronged him personally, and there was no place for them to run.

On December 7, 1993, Colin Ferguson bought an eastbound ticket to Long Island at the Brooklyn station near where he was living. After transferring trains at Penn Station, Ferguson boarded the third car of the eastbound train for Hicksville.

Just before the train reached the Merrilon Avenue Station, Ferguson began methodically walking towards the front of the car, shooting the white and Asian passengers in the process.

Almost immediately, the passengers realized what was happening and began to panic, causing a stampede that injured even more commuters.

Ferguson was able to empty two fifteen-round clips into twenty-five people in an approximately three minute span.

Finally, heroic passengers Mike O'Connor, Kevin Blum, and Mark McEntee wrestled Ferguson to the ground and took his weapon.

More passengers may have been saved, but once the situation became known to the Long Island Rail Road authorities, they ordered the doors to remain closed. Engineer Thomas Silhan ignored the order, climbed out of his cab, and then opened the doors of the car manually.

A Most Bizarre Trial

Once Colin Ferguson's massacre became public, a continuum of emotions were felt across the country from fear to anger. As elected officials tried to ease racial tensions in order to avoid reprisal attacks, it soon became clear to the Nassau County district attorney that Ferguson's murder trial would take on a circus-like atmosphere.

The case against Ferguson appeared open and shut: he killed his victims in front of plenty of witnesses and there were several anti-white statements he publically made that would go to prove motive.

But then famed leftist attorneys William Kunstler and Ron Kuby took the case.

Kunstler was noted for taking on many notable defendants, such as a prisoner in the 1971 Attica prison riot, during the 1960s and '70s. During the 1980s, he took Ron Kuby under his wing as his protégé and the duo became known for some rather eccentric defense techniques.

For Ferguson's defense, they argued that the Jamaican immigrant was driven insane from racism and that he was in fact the victim of "black rage."

The defense earned widespread dismissal by people across the United States who were following the case on the Court TV network. The defense was definitely unorthodox, but the reality was it was all they had.

And Ferguson was not willing to cooperate!

He fired Kunstler and Kuby and decided to represent himself during the trial.

The case proved to be one of the most entertaining and bizarre trials ever televised. Ferguson constantly referred to himself in third person, cross examined survivors with non-sequitur questions, and took the stand in his own defense.

While on the stand, Ferguson's explanations for the shooting went from the laughable to the truly bizarre. At first, he claimed that he was asleep during the shooting and that the true shooter planted the gun on him. He later claimed that a chip was implanted in his head by Asian scientists and that the Jewish Defense League was trying to kill him.

The jury wasted little time in deliberating and quickly came back with a guilty verdict on February 17, 1995. Ferguson was given a life sentence without the possibility of parole and was sent to the notoriously violent Attica state prison in upstate New York.

The Aftermath of the Shooting

Colin Ferguson's three minutes of carnage on the Long Island commuter train left deep scars across the country that have yet to heal and even behind bars Ferguson continues to feel the effects of his shooting spree.

Ferguson has not been one of the most popular inmates in the New York Department of Corrections. His beliefs and actions immediately put him at odds with the white inmates. While still awaiting trial in Nassau County, Ferguson was beaten by a group of white inmates and he has also experienced problems with inmates in Attica over the last two decades.

In one notable conflict, he fought with serial killer Joel Rifkin over use of a phone.

Ferguson told the serial killer, "I wiped out six devils, and you only killed women."

"Yeah, but I had more victims," Rifkin responded.

Ferguson then punched Rifkin, which earned him a stay in the segregation unit.

There is little doubt that we have not heard the last of Colin Ferguson, even from behind bars.

The shooting also became the cause for social debates in the American media. Instead of focusing on racial tensions, most of the news stories focused on gun control. The majority of opinion pieces took a pro-control stance and some argued for a ban on hollow point bullets.

The railway shooting was used by politicians to support the 1994 Assault Weapons Ban and helped launch the political career of Carolyn McCarthy.

McCarthy's husband Dennis was killed during the attack and her son Mike survived, but sustained permanent, debilitating injuries at the crazed shooter's hands. McCarthy won a seat in the U.S. House of Representatives that she held until she retired from Congress in 2015.

Politicians at the state level in New York followed the shooting by enacting some of the most restrictive gun laws in the United States, but not everyone was in favor of more gun laws.

A reaction to the initial calls for more gun control came through talk radio personalities of the 1990s, such as G. Gordon Liddy and Rush Limbaugh, who argued that more lenient gun laws may have actually saved lives. If New Yorkers were allowed to carry firearms the talk show hosts argued, then the shooter would have been stopped much sooner.

The reality is that Colin Ferguson was an extremely deranged man with a chip the size of Texas on his shoulder. If he had not killed the commuters on that train, he would have found another place and manner in which to kill people.

No law could have stopped Colin Ferguson.

Conclusion

The twelve cases profiled in this book prove that extreme acts of violence can happen anywhere, anytime, and to anyone. Developing countries and the United States do not have a monopoly on violence.

Some of these cases, such as the Mealin Road murder, were solved through advances in science, while others like the Maurin family murder were cracked by good old-fashioned police work and a mountain of circumstantial evidence.

Unfortunately, one of the most notorious crimes discussed here, the Keddie cabin murders, remains unsolved and probably will continue to be as the primary suspects are all deceased.

If there is one thing that you can get from all of these cases is to be prepared at all times. You might be on a commuter train after work or picking your children up from school and disaster can strike in the form of a deranged person.

Keep your head up and your eyes and ears open at all times!

MORE BOOKS BY JACK ROSEWOOD

Have you checked out Jack Rosewood's bestselling Serial Killer Encyclopedia yet?

There is little more terrifying than those who hunt, stalk and snatch their prey under the cloak of darkness. These hunters search not for animals, but for the touch, taste, and empowerment of human flesh. They are cannibals, vampires and monsters, and they walk among us.

These serial killers are not mythical beasts with horns and shaggy hair. They are people living among society, going about their day to day activities until nightfall. They are the Dennis Rader's, the fathers, husbands, church going members of the community.

This A-Z encyclopedia of 150 serial killers is the ideal reference book. Included are the most famous true crime serial killers, like Jeffrey Dahmer, John Wayne Gacy, and Richard Ramirez, and not to mention the women who kill, such as Aileen Wuornos and Martha Rendell. There are also lesser known serial killers, covering many countries around the world, so the range is broad.

Each of the serial killer files includes information on when and how they killed the victims, the background of each killer, or the suspects in some cases such as the Zodiac killer, their trials and punishments. For some there are chilling quotes by the killers themselves. The Big Book of Serial Killers is an easy to follow collection of information on the world's most heinous murderers.

WARNING! The following true crime book may shock and frighten the faint hearted. In the pages of this book are assembled twelve of the strangest true crime stories in human history. There is no doubt that some of these cases will disturb you, but it is equally assured that you will not be able to put this book down!

Follow along in various criminal investigations as astute investigators race to solve cold murder cases. Some of the cases in this true crime anthology will boggle your mind as much as the police were when they investigated them. You will read about the abduction of girls from safe neighborhoods during broad daylight and how the dogged detectives eventually caught their killers through a combination of advances in science, some lucky breaks, and excellent police work. There are also some true crime murder cases profiled where killers have yet to be brought to justice and unfortunately, probably never will be. You may have already heard about some of these cases, while it will be the first time you read about others, but make no mistake, you will keep turning the pages for more.

So open the pages and read about bizarre abductions, true murder cases, and other strange crimes that have intrigued people around the world. Once you do, you will want to read more.

GET THESE BOOKS FOR FREE

Go to http://www.jackrosewood.com/free
and get this E-Book for free!

A NOTE FROM THE AUTHOR

Hello, this is Jack Rosewood. Thank you for reading this book. I hope you enjoyed the read. If you did, I'd appreciate if you would take a few moments to post a review on Amazon.

I would also love if you'd sign up to my newsletter to receive updates on new releases, promotions and a FREE copy of my Herbert Mullin E-Book, go to www.JackRosewood.com

Thanks again for reading this book, make sure to follow me on Facebook.

Best Regards
Jack Rosewood

Made in the USA
San Bernardino, CA
02 December 2017